"Awesome" is an adjective describing something that is a mixed bag of reverence, fear and wonder. Canon Davis' little book of chronicles, recounting a Chaplain's service with Canadian troops in World War II, is all this – and more. Its awesomeness is softened by the thread of soldiers' humour that made that existence bearable.

. . . The many anecdotes which pace this narrative are told in the simplicity of a line sketch. Each tells its own story, each stands alone as a part of the whole mosaic of a gunner's active service in wartime. This chronicle is a record of the triumph of Faith, recounted in demands of ministry that reveal both the integrity of the author, and the power of that Faith as it was mediated to men at war.

The Venerable P. Sidney Irwin

AN AWESOME SILENCE

A GUNNER PADRE'S JOURNEY THROUGH
THE VALLEY OF THE SHADOW

ELDON S. DAVIS

Published by
Creative Bound Inc.
P.O. Box 424, Carp, Ontario
Canada K0A 1L0

ISBN 0-921165-19-6
Printed and bound in Canada

Book Design: Wendelina O'Keefe
Cover Photo: Photographic Illustrations, Ottawa, Ontario

Canadian Cataloguing in Publication Data
Davis, Eldon S. (Eldon Stanley), 1913-

An awesome silence: a gunner padre's journey through the valley of the shadow

ISBN 0-921165-19-6

1. World War, 1939-1945 -- Personnal narratives, Canadian.
2. World War, 1939-1945 -- Chaplains -- Canada. 3. Davis, Eldon S.
(Eldon Stanley), 1913 -
I. Title

D811.D33A3 1991   940.54'78'0971092   C91-090410-3

DEDICATION

*To the Officers and Gunners with whom
I shared this baptism of pain and terror,
I humbly dedicate this little book.*

TABLE OF CONTENTS

FOREWORD

From the first hour of a post-war reunion in Ottawa, when he told you of his extraordinary experiences as a Padre with the Canadian artillery in Italy, you urged him to put them down on paper – presenting a picture of war from the special perspective on a non-combatant who shared all the usual miseries and risks of active service, while ministering to the living and burying the dead for months on end.

Blessed with a most sensitive and perceptive mind, and being a wonderful raconteur, his stories cried out for publication.

Some were very funny, and some terribly sad; some heart-rendingly poignant, and some horrifying brutal – but all told with compassion, never more apparent than when he was recalling how little resilience was given to some men to face the possibility of sudden death, and how great it was in others.

However, the years went by without any of these wonderful stories being committed to paper. The parish curate had no time or inclination in those first years in Ottawa after the war to spend on memoirs. Then there was even less time as a missionary in India responsible for a leprosy clinic and rehabilitation centre at Palampur, where he met and married a lovely nurse from Australia, and his responsibilities grew as his family grew.

Back in Ottawa, fifteen years later, there were all the pressures of a new parish, the building of a new church, and the ever-increasing demands for his services as a counsellor – particularly by the young in the bewildering 60s and 70s – demands that grew so extensive, the diocese came to recognize the need and help him set up a six-day a week counselling service at the Cathedral.

While realizing that untold numbers benefited profoundly from counselling received from this wise and understanding man, you were plagued with the idea that memory might fail before he had his stories down on paper. Finally, however, on retirement he got down to it and this fine little volume is the result.

The content of the odd story may shock some who have not known the horrors of the battlefield, or the effects of long years of "active service" on the lives of men and women separated by thousands of miles for up to six years. But there is an ennobling quality shining through all his narratives which is the essence of the man, for Padre Eldon Davis was a real man, when real men counted – a consistent Christian regardless of whom he was with or how dreadful were the conditions – unfailingly tolerant of other mens' weaknesses, but never willing to countenance weakness in himself, or allow himself to be bullied by authoritarians regardless of which side of the war they were on.

George G. Blackburn M.C.

1

ON THE WAY TO WAR

In 1939, I was only six weeks out of Seminary when I was sent to the parish of Petawawa, a few miles north of Pembroke, Ontario. Part of my duties was to be padre to the militia batteries who came from all over Ontario to Petawawa Military Camp for periods of training each summer.

When war broke out in September, I was asked by a retired permanent force officer when I would be joining the active forces; thus I was moved to investigate the process. After all, it wasn't just a matter of reporting to a recruiting centre. I was somewhat dismayed, however, when I discovered one of the requirements of entering the chaplain service as a padre was five years experience in parish work.

Bishop Wells, the Chaplain General, on a visit to Petawawa Camp, came to Pembroke and spoke at Trinity Church, my parish church. I had intended to ask him if I could get into the services a bit early, but he had such unkind words to say from the pulpit about the younger generation, I decided against the move. But after he'd been in England and bombed out of his house in London, he returned to Petawawa with a different outlook. He told me "This is a young man's war!" and asked me why I was not in uniform. I sent in my application right away and was accepted.

My last parish duty was to fulfill a promise to an old man, Mr. John Dole. I skied in to his home on the banks of the Ottawa River which is now the site of the town of Deep River. He and his wife lived in a spacious one-room log cabin, the inside of which was covered entirely with birch bark. His wife was an Indian woman of great dignity. She had set up a small table to serve as an altar, and had candles burning on it, which seemed to me far too close to the birch bark wall; only about eight inches separated the candles from the tinder-dry bark in the room that was kept at about eighty-five degrees fahrenheit.

However, we proceeded and after the Eucharist ended, Mr. Dole invited me to stay for lunch. His wife, who was ninety-two (two years older than her husband) took down a twenty-two calibre rifle from a nail, and throwing a shawl over her shoulders went out. In about fifteen minutes she returned carrying three limp, ruffled grouse. To my surprise I noted all three had been shot through the head! When I questioned her husband he just said, "My wife has never ruined her eyes by reading."

When I was on the point of leaving, after a delicious lunch of roasted grouse, Mr. Dole remarked that his wife was "sad" that I was going away. I took her by the hand and said, "Mrs. Dole, when I come back from the war, I will come and see you."

She replied, "You will come back, but I shall not be here."

It was the most she had ever said during the time I had

known her.

The old man came outside with me, and taking my hand said, "My wife is very sad seeing you off to war. You see, we had five sons and two of them fell at Vimy Ridge and Passchendaele."

As she prophesied, I came back and she was gone. Throughout my service in action, as I took care of the burial of other mothers' sons, I often recalled her loving, old face and felt her pain for her fallen sons.

The memories of my good-byes to my family were jumbled together like a pile of Christmas cards. Events like these are painful, and so, in an odd sort of way, it was a relief when the train moved out of Ottawa Union Station.

In Montreal we were delayed for several hours while two huge trainloads of troops moved out ahead of us toward "an Eastern Canadian port." The interval allowed me to call my cousin, Ruth Swan, and promise to take her greetings to her husband who was already in England. This beautiful lady rushed down to the station, arriving just as our train began to move out. Running after it, she just managed to hand a large fruit cake to a young officer at the end of the train. He came along until he found and identified me. It was a loving gift.

Halifax was a seething, amorphous mob of uniforms, moving at the command of a blaring loudspeaker. Many of us were not moving as particular units, so we were seated in front of huge black numbers. These numbers seemed to be all important; in fact, they seemed to be the only identification which mattered at all. An order would come over the P.A. telling number twenty-six to move, and all the uniforms by that number would rise, butt out cigarettes, pick up kit bags, and move on board ship under the direction of an N.C.O. (Non-Commissioned Officer).

Two officers met near where I was sitting. One of them used an expression quite new to me then, but one I was to hear often in the next four years. "I need fifty-three bodies," he said. The other, pointing to a number, said, "I have fifty-one there." The first replied, "That will do."

The fifty-one bodies moved woodenly as they were directed on board ship. When our order came, our sixty-three bodies moved aboard just as the group before us had done. Most soldiers have numbers which are their identity, but for this operation the only number that mattered was the big one surrounded by khaki-uniformed bodies. It was a strange phenomenon. None of us knew the names of the other bodies in our group. I could imagine how prisoners felt as they boarded trains taking them to a new prison camp. An awful sense of anonymity hung over us until we boarded our transport.

Just before this happened I observed another phenomenon of war – the effect of new and sudden changes in the lives of soldiers and their loved ones. A tearful goodbye took place close to where I sat between two young officers and two beautiful young ladies, whom I surmised were their wives or sweethearts. It was indeed a touching farewell. When the last good-byes had been said and the officers walked smartly aboard the troopship, the two ladies ordered cups of tea at a service booth. They were presently joined by two N.C.O.s who were not embarking. After a while the party became somewhat relaxed and they moved off the dock arm in arm. Such were the strange effects of war.

Our ship, called the *Andes,* had been built for traffic on the River Plate and had a very shallow keel, necessary for travel on that South American river, but not too appropriate for the stormy North Atlantic.

We awakened next morning after leaving Halifax to find ourselves under the protection of a battleship, two cruisers and twelve destroyers of the American Navy. I felt a wave of emotion that that great nation, while officially neutral, was in reality guarding our safety on the high seas. It was an awesome array of power.

Then, one day out from Great Britain, we awakened to find the American escorts had disappeared as they had come, in the darkness of night. (Although the Americans had not yet declared war, they had lost two destroyers in previous escort duty in October.) Far out on the horizon we could make out the forms of four small camouflaged destroyers of the British Navy, barely visible in the early morning light. Strangely enough, we felt no less safe under the protection of the four tiny ships manned by Nelson's sailors.

One night after dinner, I went out on the darkened deck; it was a scary experience. Earlier in the day the ship's captain told me the prow of the *Andes* was pitching sixty feet with each wave. In addition to this, a notice had been posted earlier in the day that anyone going out on an open deck did so at his own risk. It was further stated that if anyone fell overboard, a rescue attempt would not be made and life preservers would not be dropped. Nevertheless, the sheer danger held me like a spell.

I was brought back to reality when someone dashed past me to the rail and promptly lost his dinner. The effect of my being on the leeward side of him was so drastic that, although up to that time I had felt fine, I dashed after him to the rail for a similar reason and the same result. At that moment, the big ship lurched forward and then heeled over to an extreme angle, throwing both of us heavily against the steel rail. My companion of the moment cried

13

out with fear. He was desperately afraid of falling to the deck and being tossed through the steel bars, into the black water, thirty feet below. So was I. This horrendous thought gave us strength through terror. We waited for a somewhat more even keel and made a dash for the doorway, about eight feet away, which would take us below deck and to relative safety.

Once inside, I offered to go to the galley and get us some sandwiches and tea. But my partner just sat on a box of life preservers, and, holding his head with both hands, slowly moved it from side to side. For the remainder of the voyage I stayed below deck at night.

A Brigadier appointed me as an Orderly Officer. He told me that, while he would look after the officers, my job would be to liaise with all other ranks in matters concerning food. My work was somewhat simplified by the fact that fifty percent of the men were deathly sick and had very little interest in food. That percentage was increased dramatically when the survivors were served their first breakfast – a huge and deathly cold baked potato. When I commented on this, one soldier started to address his potato, "How can we possibly convince the padre that you received the last rites of the church before we left Halifax? The shameful thing is, noone even asked you if you had any objections to being buried at sea".

I went to the galley and quickly conceded that cooking was not possible. Instead, I suggested that the cooks make up bully beef sandwiches to serve with tea and coffee. This, along with fruits and sweets, and plum and apple jam sandwiches, was to be the menu for most of the voyage. My close association with the galley so imprinted itself on my mind that I hoped if I didn't make it to heaven, I might at least avoid being assigned as galley cook on some flat-bottomed Stygian vessel.

Each night at dinner I attended the officers' mess, sitting opposite the Brigadier. This officer was always getting new ideas, one of which was to have chicken gumbo soup because it didn't splash easily. For this operation he chose the night of the heaviest seas I have ever witnessed in my lifetime. The waiters had miraculously placed the eight bowls of soup on the table without mishap, when our crazy ship had her bow lifted up at a frightening angle and plunged deep in an oncoming wave. The Brigadier, sitting facing the bow, had his chair pulled to the full length of the chain anchoring it to the floor. In a reflex action he grasped the end of the table, including the edge of his soup bowl. This, in turn, along with the motion of the ship, flipped the bowl over and deposited its contents on his uniform just under his chin. In horror, we watched the thick chicken gumbo ooze slowly down over his red collar tabs.

Noting the vulnerability of my exposed position, I stood up, bowed to my senior officer, picked up my bowl of soup and moved quickly to the exit. As I passed the trash can at the door, I dropped the chicken gumbo into it. Not one officer noted my exit. This cowardly retreat to the chaos of the galley gave rise to a new proverb: "He who laughs and runs away shall live to laugh another day." The story, which preceded me to the galley, produced an outburst of mirth among the cooks who had laboured to produce the Brigadier's gumbo. Since that fateful night, I have never had chicken gumbo soup.

We arrived in Southampton in darkness and heavy cloud cover. We were soon entrained for Aldershot, where I was sent to holding unit #1 C.A.R.U. Bordon, Hants.

2

A COURT MARTIAL

It was in Hants that I had my first experience with a court martial. I was asked to serve on the board with two majors, the usual number of officers in such a court. I was slightly put off at the outset by one of these gentlemen who, when I asked a question, replied, "Padre, don't bother yourself with these military matters. We'll tell you what to do." Under my breath, I whispered, "Major, we may have some rough weather ahead."

The prisoner was seventeen years old; he had enlisted when he was fifteen. It appeared he had been fifteen minutes late getting back from Farnham. The conductress had put her arm across the entrance to the bus just in front of him, and the next bus got him into Aldershot at 12:15 midnight. He was charged with being AWOL (absent without official leave).

Brought before the commanding officer, he was asked why he was late, and he told the story of the bus episode. The Colonel, making a little speech, concluded with the question, "What would happen if I was always fifteen minutes late?"

To this the prisoner replied, "But sir, I haven't got a staff car."

The Colonel's voice took on a hard note. "Will you take my punishment?" The boy assented and the Colonel continued. "Twenty-eight days CB (confined to barracks). Next case." I heard later that the Colonel had been nicknamed, Colonel February. When I enquired why, I was asked if I hadn't noticed how nicely he had said "twenty-eight days."

While serving his sentence in the regimental guardhouse, the prisoner had found he was being charged nineteen dollars for a greatcoat he had lent a friend working in a nearby office. So, when the prisoner was allowed to walk outside for exercise, he had decided to extend his walk a hundred yards farther and retrieve the coat. He had been picked up by the military police for being on the street without a forage cap. The sergeant at the guardhouse was reprimanded by his officer, and he, in turn, leaned rather heavily on the prisoner who then retaliated by punching the sergeant on the nose. This had led to the court martial.

During the trial, I pleaded for leniency due to the age of the prisoner and extenuating circumstances, particularly in connection with the original charge. The chairman of the court looked at me with disgust and said, "So our padre is a bleeding heart." Then, with incredible petulance, he added, "Padre, just to show my heart is in the right place, I'm going to increase the sentence from eighteen months to two years in the glasshouse. All in favour?" There was majority assent, and the boy was sentenced to two years in this infamous detention centre. The glasshouse was a prison where the incarcerated were subjected to what could be described as organized torment. According to another member of the Third Field who had served one year there, prisoners were often wakened after midnight by an N.C.O., telling them he smelled smoke, and demanding a kit inspection. This meant that bedding, clothing, toilet articles and, indeed, all possessions, had to be laid out for inspection. Their tormentor then picked up their palliases (denim bags filled with straw) and shook out all the straw onto their kit, presumably looking for cigarettes. They were then told to put the straw back in their mattress covers and to clean up the whole place without the convenience of a broom. Soon after getting back to bed, they were awakened again and the whole operation was repeated. This was just one way guards used to humiliate and demoralize the prisoners.

One would suppose that the purpose of all this was to discourage men from wanting to return to the glasshouse, and certainly it did tend to have that effect. However, the idea of volunteer soldiers and fellow countrymen being subjected to treatment which would be universally condemned by the civilized world seemed to me a repugnant thing. Until the time of my first and only service on a court martial, I hadn't any idea such an institution operated under the aegis of the army. The more I learned about the glasshouse, the more confirmed I became that this type of punishment was highly questionable. Even given the fact that we were fighting for our lives and freedom, and that in the early days there wasn't any certainty of victory, this was a shameful institution and one which I fervently hope will never be used again by our armed forces.

I called the Senior Chaplain in London, explained the circumstances and asked him to try to have the boy discharged from the Army on compassionate grounds – he was still under nineteen, the legal age for service outside of Canada. After informing the Colonel of my appeal for action, I had the prisoner retained at the regiment until the order came through for his return to Canada. The leader of the court martial was, to say the least, not pleased, and he expressed some strange and largely unprintable hopes and predictions about my future in the army.

3

STRANGER THAN FICTION

Very late one evening, while I was still in Hants, a man came to see me. He was deeply disturbed and informed me that he had not slept for more than seventy-two hours. Moreover, each time he began to tell me his trouble he would dissolve into tears. He kept repeating that somehow he had to get out of the hell he was in. "Padre," he said, "I know I have to do something, but I don't know what and I don't know how. I think I'm going crazy."

I put my arms around him and held him in a solid grip until he stopped crying, and I suggested he start at the beginning and tell me the story.

I was surprised when he told me it started in World War I, as I had assumed he was about my own age. But he was ten years older than I; he had lied about his age and joined up when he was fifteen. He was sent to England and celebrated his sixteenth birthday there as the war drew to a close.

Shortly after arriving in England he had met an attractive English girl and kept company with her for several months. This was the happiest time of his life, he said. They planned to get married and come to Canada at the end of the war. It was at this particular time that matters took a turn for the worse.

The war ended with dramatic suddenness, and at the same time, his friend discovered that she was pregnant. The young soldier applied for permission to marry. But the rush to get veterans home to Canada – some of whom had been away from home for nearly five years – gave those in authority little time for, or interest in, the problems of this very young couple. The soldier was quickly moved to Southampton, loaded on a transport, shipped to Halifax and then on to Winnipeg. The processes of war had torn the couple apart, leaving the boy helpless and frustrated, and his loved one desperate and alone in an unthinking world. Fear caused her to hide her condition from her family, and her despair was intensified by stories of other girls who had become pregnant and were left behind by uncaring soldiers.

Then something happened which further complicated the situation. The boy next door came back from the Far East to find the gangling little girl he had known, very grown up and beautiful. He fell in love with her and asked her to marry him. She bravely told him she didn't love him, but the soldier replied that he loved her enough for both of them. Her parents were delighted.

It now became almost impossible for her to tell her family the truth. In quiet despair she accepted the marriage proposal. The wedding took place two weeks after she had written a final letter to her Canadian telling him of her decision and asking him not to write to her again. He honoured her request. Seven months later the baby was born and it was assumed it was 'born early'.

The years went by and the boy in Canada grew to a man. He often thought of the past. The quiet ache of memory sometimes bothered him as he lay awake in the small hours of the morning. He had thought of marriage, but the care of his parents and the straitened circumstances of the Depression years made it impossible.

When his parent died, he enlisted and was sent with the First Canadian Division to Britain. A few months later he met an attractive English girl and went out with her for about six months before being invited to visit her parents in London. He accepted the invitation with enthusiasm, for the past six months had been one of the happiest periods of his life. He got a seventy-two-hour leave, and he and his girl set out for London, their hearts filled with happiness.

They arrived at her home to find her father present. He said his wife was doing volunteer work and would be home in a few hours. The two men shared a deep interest in ecology, and her father was fascinated by the experiences of the Canadian. The father also had a second hobby – he was an amateur clockmaker, and during the war he had begun to repair clocks for close friends and neighbours. He asked his daughter to help him carry the weights and chains of a grandfather clock back to a neighbour who lived several blocks away. The Canadian was left reading some notes on 'hedge ecology'.

The pair had scarcely left the house when her mother returned. They met in the living room, recognizing each other immediately. She saw the desperate question in his eyes. Without a word she slowly nodded her head, laid her hand on the stricken man's arm and said, in a low voice, "Your regiment called, and you were ordered to return immediately."

He nodded his reply. They stood in silence for a few long minutes. Then, shaking away the tears, they embraced briefly, and the Canadian hurried away.

As he turned the corner, he looked back to see the mother standing in the open door. His heart broke as he pondered upon the immensely difficult situation the poor woman was in, having to explain to their daughter why he had so abruptly disappeared.

4

A QUESTION OF DIVORCE

At least fifty percent of the problems, presented by men seeking advice and help, sprang from marital relations or non-marital liaisons. Very frequently, I had soldiers come and ask me how one went about starting procedures for a divorce. I would answer that first of all we would want to be sure he wanted a divorce.

One soldier, responding with annoyance, told me that his wife was having a baby – a year and a half after he had left Canada. "Besides, Padre," he concluded, "she has asked for a divorce."

Acknowledging that that was serious, but detecting some hesitance in his voice, I asked him to give me a few weeks to look into the matter. I discovered by questioning further that he still loved his wife.

Soon after, I wrote to her, telling her that I believed Jim still loved her, and asking her to fill me in on the details. In a short time I received her reply. It was a beautiful and touching letter:

Padre, I received your letter and I have never laid it down since it arrived. It represents the only hope I have for my future.

When I learned that I was pregnant I went to my mother-in-law and sister-in-law. They were very hostile. They told me the only decent thing to do was to write James and ask for a divorce. They said it was not enough to offer him a divorce – I should ask for it. That is why I wrote to him as I did, and asked for a divorce I didn't want.

Four months ago a dance was arranged for troops who were leaving for England. My sister-in-law and a mutual friend asked me to go, as there was a severe shortage of girls for the dance. They assured me that it would be all right and that they would go with me and bring me home as well. I was a little uncomfortable when a very nice soldier asked me to dance and then came and sat with me after it ended. From then on, he asked me for every dance. My two companions waved to me a couple of times and then proceeded to go their own way. My friend came to me and told me she knew the boy who was dancing with me and that he had his father's car and would drive me home.

The fact that I didn't put my foot down then was a mark of my immaturity, if not stupidity. When the dance ended he drove me home, and I offered to make a cup of cocoa, which he accepted. Then, when he was saying good-bye, he kissed me – that kiss lasted for four hours.

You might well ask how a woman who loves her husband could get into such a situation, and I have to say I don't know the answer myself. I only know that a year and a half of being alone with two small children had not prepared me to be in close and intimate contact with a very gentle and considerate man. Had he been the obvious type, the situation would never have arisen.

He left for Europe the next day, and I have, of course, never heard from him again. Despite all of this, he was gentle and considerate. I attach no blame to him, even though I realize it was those two attributes which made me vulnerable.

Padre, in spite of all this, will you believe me that I still love my husband with all my heart?

When my friend heard about the pregnancy she told me she knew of a doctor who performed abortions. She urged me to go to him before my sister-in-law learned of the situation. I replied that I might be a bad woman, but I was not a murderer. She went away in a huff and, I believe, gave the news to my sister-in-law.

I took the letter to her soldier husband and let him read it. His reaction was startling. He burst out, "How dare they? How dare they say that to my wife! I'll wipe the floor with them!"

Then he wrote to his wife, told her that he loved her more than ever and that he was proud of her for refusing to have an abortion. He was also prepared to keep the baby. I told him that while I was not opposed to this, I felt I must draw his attention to some of the potential problems. For instance, it would be quite impossible to hide the child's birth circumstances when the child grew up. There was also the possibility that some malicious person might give him or her the information beforehand. I also warned him that this could create tension in the family and in himself. "It's not impossible," I concluded, "but it's very tricky."

Eventually, when I was leaving the Holding Unit to join my regiment, he happened to be on guard duty at the gate. I asked him to stand at ease and we had a little talk. As I departed, he said, "Padre, we may never meet again, but I want you to know you will always be a most important person in our lives. I will remember that you saved my life and my world. Good-bye, my friend."

5

THE THIRD FIELD REGIMENT

Early in 1942 I was posted to the Third Field Regiment, a field artillery unit using twenty-five-pounders. They supported the Second Brigade and were composed of the three infantry regiments and support units. In practice, the three artillery regiments could be called upon to support one infantry regiment if it was in trouble.

I had been with my new regiment only a few hours when I received a call from a girl in London. She was very distressed. She told me she was to be married on Friday of that week but hadn't heard from her fiance for two weeks. Further to this, the wedding dress was bought, the wedding cake had been prepared and her relatives from northern England were due to arrive in a day or so.

I told her I was new to the regiment and, therefore, didn't know her fiance, but I promised to find out what I could and call her. I discovered that the soldier was out on two days of manoeuvres and would not be back until late in the evening. However, I obtained from his battery the information that he was married and his wife was in Winnipeg with their two children. Deciding that drastic and immediate action was imperative, I went up to London to have a talk with the girl and her family. I told them what I had discovered, and advised them to take immediate steps to stop the wedding and save their relatives from the expense and futility of a journey to London.

Discussing the matter with her father, I discovered a strange and, to me, totally inexplicable, slant to the saga. He told me that he had pleaded with the bombardier to postpone the wedding for a year. He had told his daughter, "You are only nineteen and there isn't any compelling reason for you to rush this wedding." To his surprise, it was not his daughter who opposed delay, but his son-in-law to be. He put up a spirited argument to have the wedding as soon as possible. The father continued, "I cannot understand why he was so vehemently opposed to the delay. It just doesn't make any sense to me."

When the soldier returned to his regiment, I invited him to come to my office. I had a number of questions to ask him, including the one which so puzzled the girl's father. "Bombardier, you have a wife and two children in Winnipeg?" I began.

"Yes, Padre."

"You are not intending to divorce your wife?"

"No, I'm not."

"I note that you arranged a wedding for tomorrow. Could you tell me why this happened?"

"Well, Padre, it was one of those things that creep up on you."

"Bombardier, I did note that your girlfriend is very attractive, but what puzzles her father and me is why you have allowed this matter to advance to this stage before putting a stop to it."

"Padre," he answered, "I know I should have stopped it. But the truth is, she was having such a good time getting ready for the wedding, I didn't have the heart to stop her."

I had to admit that this was certainly a novel excuse. I called the girl concerned to come to our regimental headquarters and suggested that the bombardier pay for the wedding preparations. He winced a little but promised to do so. I surrendered my office entirely to both of them and suggested that they come up with a figure in an hour or so.

During this time, I talked with the bombardier's gun crew, and they informed me that two of them had warned the lady that her boyfriend was married, but she had refused to believe them.

After waiting nearly two hours, I knocked loudly and opened the door. They appeared to have just awakened from a sound sleep on my small and uncomfortable couch. Once again, I surrendered to the unusual, retreating to that catch-all French expression, "Ce n'est rien; c'est la guerre."

The bombardier's comrades chipped in and lent him the money to cover the cost of the wedding. One of them even offered an explanation for the episode on the couch: "Padre, I suppose you could call that saying good-bye with style!"

6

PETS

During the years I was with the Third Field Regiment, I can remember only one period when we didn't have pets – that was during the invasion of Sicily. In England, there was the cat who thought she was a dog, walked like a dog and would have no truck or trade with other cats. But if the convoy stopped for five minutes in an English village and she saw a dog lying in his owner's garden, she would jump down from her perch in the vehicle and make a beeline for the canine. She would then pick a fight with him, a fight she always seemed to win.

Supposedly, a cat is home-oriented – not this one! She was a real gypsy. The gun crew was her family and she was ready to move day or night. She had her perch in what is known as the gun tractor or quad. I never knew what happened to her when we left Britain for the invasion of Sicily.

Then, there was the dog called 'Bones'. In the town of West Wickham, he became a legend with the local bus company. Every Saturday night, his master, Sgt. Jones, made his way to one of the three local pubs and spent the evening in the peace and quiet of one of those great

English institutions. Well before closing time, Bones would bestir himself, leave his home beside Sgt. Jones' bedroll and board the local double-decker bus, where he took his accustomed place under the stairway. Then, leaping off at the first pub, he would follow someone inside, look around, and if his master was not there, he would go out and wait for the next bus to take him to the second stop. Some peevish bus clippie (conductor) might chase him off the bus, whereupon he would wait for the next bus and go on to the second pub. If he didn't find Jones there, he would go on to the third. Finally locating his master, he would nudge him with a wet nose, and Jones would say, "So you've come to take me home, lad. Well let's go." And off they would go to the billet where they laid down their heads.

One day, while we were out on manoeuvres, Bones wanted to cross a track on the moors. He waited for a bus on his right to pass and trotted out as it passed him. But he failed to look to the left and walked out into the path of a lorry. He was killed instantly. The C.O. commented, "I'm glad I'm not in competition with Bones and have to depend on who would get the most votes in the regiment to go on living." I was moved to write this little poem:

> *Here's to a dog by the name of Bones,*
> *The beloved friend of Sgt. Jones.*
> *Truly a mechanized pup was he,*
> *For in jeep and bus he travelled free.*
> *But a lorry ran over poor old Bones,*
> *And our hearts go out to Sgt. Jones.*
> *How he'll get back now from his weekly spree,*
> *Is something we'll just have to wait and see.*

7

ON GARRISON DUTY ON THE CHANNEL

Just after I joined the Third Field Regiment, I received a telegram from my sister informing me of the death of my mother. It was one of the blackest times of my life. My eldest brother had been killed at Passchendaele in the First World War, and years after his death I would, from time to time, see my mother weeping over the death of her first-born child. My joining the army must have been an added burden. She died three months after I arrived in Britain.

When I was called to the orderly room to receive the telegram, our adjutant was not present. As I returned to my billet, I passed him on the other side of the street. I suppose I gave him a small return to his cheery greeting, and in a few minutes, he was back to my house with a very brusque order.

"Padre, a staff car will take you to the train station in twenty minutes. You have a pass and rail tickets to any place in Britain, and you have seven days' leave starting now. Hurry it up, Padre." And he gave me a small punch in the chest. I was grateful for his caring brusqueness.

On the train, I met for the first time an extraordinary

family, who took me into their home in Manchester and made life bearable for three days. From there I went on to Yorkshire, where I was received with love into the community of an Anglican monastery. The Brothers let me work with them in the fields and pray with them in their lovely chapel. During the day, there was complete silence, but from supper until the Service of Compline, they talked with gentleness and loving care. I returned to my regiment healed in body and spirit.

The First Division, one of the few divisions equipped with twenty-five-pounders (the British had lost all of theirs at Dunkirk), was placed along the vulnerable section of the Coast of Sussex. It was situated there to help repel the expected German assault in the late summer and early fall of 1940. When I joined Third Field in early 1942, they were still there, having been joined by Second Division.

From then until 1943, when the Division was pulled out for special training in Scotland to prepare for shipping out to the Mediterranean and the invasion of Sicily, the Third Field participated in an endless number of 'schemes' (army manoeuvres simulating battles) and training shoots with live ammunition. These were held at Alfriston, on Salisbury Plain, and at Senneybridge in the mountains of Wales.

It was always during the winter that the Canadian artillery was allowed training in Senneybridge. So, early in 1943, the three Field Artillery Regiments of the First Division went to the Senneybridge Artillery Range in Wales to shoot.

There, I witnessed 'scotch mist' for the first time. It was just above the freezing point, but deathly cold. I went for a long walk over the moors, and at the end of the walk

I was surprised to find that I was unable to bend my elbows to take my hands out of my pockets. I still don't know whether it was a psychological or physical phenomenon. At the time, I was passing close to a house on the edge of the moor. Approaching the door, I tapped on it with my toe. When someone answered it, I said, "I am Captain Davis, a Canadian, and I would like to warm myself for a little while at your fire." The man asked me in, turned, and said to the people gathered there, "He is one of us." To me, he added, "We are having a sing." I hastened to warn these Welsh people that I was no songbird, whatever my name. (I didn't reveal that my origins were mostly Scottish and Irish.)

These kind folk gave me a warm welcome. I saw hams and bacon hanging from the ceiling – a bounty not found in any part of Britain I had visited. They plied me with beautiful homemade bread, cheese and Devonshire cream, which looked like slightly soft butter. Along with this came some of the best ham I had ever tasted. I was surprised how quickly the afternoon passed. Finally, I excused myself and started back to the Regiment. On the way, my path converged with that of our Commanding Officer. He was shivering with cold, and when we arrived at the Mess he called for the Mess Sergeant, and said, "Martin, the Padre and I are half-frozen – make us a hot toddy." Then he turned to me and warned, "You have to be careful taking this on an empty stomach, Padre." I almost choked as I replied, "I'll be very careful, sir." I felt a little guilty.

Our garrison guard duty position, on the coast of Sussex, was close to the site of the last successful foreign invasion. One day, I decided to visit Battle Hill, above Hastings. Unimpressed, I went down to the sea and booked a room for the night at a local pub in the town.

As I was returning to my pub, planning to play a few games of darts, I heard the sound of fighter planes. When I looked back, I saw a formation of Messerschmitts coming in very low over the sea. Then I heard the rattle of machine gun fire, and I quickly backed up against a doorway. The machine gun and cannon fire roared past, leaving me totally terrified.

Standing with my back to the door, I grasped the knob, pulling myself as close to the door as possible. Suddenly it opened and swung inward, and I landed on my back on the floor. An English voice called out, "Who's there?" I made some meaningless remark like, "It's me." The voice instructed me to crawl to the 'Anderson', referring to a makeshift air raid shelter, a steel table under which was a mattress. There I discovered a young mother and her son, who was nearly two years of age.

After some time the 'all clear' sounded, and I said good-bye and started back to the Red Lion. I had barely reached the door when another formation of enemy planes swept in from the sea. This flight carried small bombs, one of which landed on the street a hundred feet away from my former refuge. A large fragment crashed into the door frame a few feet from me. I turned the knob and re-entered the house, scrambling into the shelter. After a long time the 'all clear' sounded, and once again I prepared to go back to my pub. By now it was quite dark, and I was in no way clear as to the way back. Finally my companion said, "It could be serious if you get lost. No one will take you in after dark. We have been warned that spies might be landed from a submarine, and told not to admit anyone after dark."

The young lady then made a suggestion. "I trust you

will not mistake my purpose if I invite you to stay here until morning. It really would be quite dangerous for you to try to find your way back to your lodging tonight." I replied that I was grateful for her kind invitation, and that she was as safe as a church. Later, I remembered all of the burnt-out churches I had seen in London and wondered how comforting my words really were to the young lady.

Before I went to sleep, I concluded that, while it would be an awkward situation to explain to one's Bishop, it was definitely better than being mistaken for a spy. I awakened in the morning and left her sleeping, easily finding my way back to my pub. I had, in fact, remembered the four turns correctly – it was the Red Lion.

8

TO SICILY VIA SCOTLAND

Over the fall and winter of 1942-43, there followed an endless round of schemes and training camps. Invariably, it was cold and wet when the Regiment was out in the open and away from billets.

The Division had been passed over for the Dieppe Raid in August 1942, and this placed a strain on morale over Christmas. It was also the fourth Christmas away from Canada.

But finally, in 1943, the eternal rumours of going into action seemed to be more authentic. The Division was moved away from the South Coast to Scotland, to practise sea-landing exercises. These turned out to be infinitely more difficult and dangerous than the actual landings that took place later in Sicily and Italy.

About two weeks before we put out to sea, a gunner came to me with an urgent problem. Sometime earlier, while he was in England, he had met a Scottish girl. He had asked for permission to marry her, but the process had been held up by red tape. Now, with his departure imminent, he wanted to know if it could be expedited so they could be married before he left the U.K. I realized that the delay had been far too long, and I made a strong appeal on behalf of the couple but to no avail. The reason had become clear – it was a matter of security. I then made a plea to the C.O. to give the soldier a five-day leave. This was granted, and I told the couple they could have their honeymoon now and get married when we returned to Britain. They took their leave, keeping in touch with us by telephone.

The boy concerned was later killed in Italy, and I had the painful task of writing his espoused wife. To my amazement, I received a very brave and beautiful letter. She thanked me for securing them permission to have five days leave together before we embarked for the Mediterranean. She wrote:

Those five days were the most beautiful of my life. I care nothing that I can't claim dependence allowance – that is of no importance. I am, of course, devastated by the death of my beloved, but had we not had those five precious days, I would have been devastated and poor as well. Instead, I know that no one can ever take that memory away from me. Padre, I will always remember that without your effort the five-day leave would not have happened. Thank you, especially for the beautiful little blessing you gave us.

The First Division sailed from Greenock Harbour. We didn't have any idea where we were going, which meant that every soldier in the great convoy could argue vehemently that he knew our exact destination. As we waited for covering darkness, the sun came out just before it set, silhouetting the islands which lay to the west. At that auspicious moment, a lone piper began to play "The Road to the Isles."

*For by Tummel and Loch Rannoch and Loch
Arber I will go
By heather banks wi' heaven in their wiles
And if it's thinking in your inner heart,
braggart's in my step
Then you've never smelt the tangle o' the Isles.*

I thought of my ancestor, a trooper in the Scots' Greys, who had fought under Wellington at Waterloo. His brother, a fellow trooper, was killed. My ancestor searched all the next day until he found his body, and he buried it after retrieving his brother's few possessions. One of these possessions was a watch that I later inherited.

And I thought of another body I'd buried. It was my first experience conducting a burial for a casualty of enemy action – a boy who died, near where we were stationed, from wounds received at Dieppe.

All the day before, there'd been the sound of heavy gunfire. But on that morning all was quiet.

At the end of the service, another lone piper had played a heartrending Scottish lament called, "The Flowers of the Forest." Our thoughts went across the seas to our "New Scotland" in Canada, where a family would be bravely trying to cope with the overwhelming loss of a son, a brother, a husband. I had to pinch my thigh to get control and give the final blessing. As I looked into the eyes of the burial party, I knew I was not the only one who had to struggle for control. When the boys had filled in the grave, and someone laid a little bouquet of English bluebells on the damp earth, I found myself repeating some lines from the "Burial of Sir John Moore":

Slowly and sadly, we laid him down
On the field of his fame, fresh and gory
We carved not a line, we raised not a stone
But we left him alone in his glory.

As we sailed out of the Clyde, bound for action, we wondered how many of these, our comrades, we would have to bury in the months ahead.

When we wakened next morning under heavy skies, we were heading due west, zig-zagging our way along. An officer, who knew something about navigation, calculated that we were sailing towards the coast of Labrador. We were still maintaining to this course four or five days later. Presently we received official word that we were going to the Mediterranean to join the Eighth Army for an attack on Sicily and Italy.

By chance, I heard the news before it was announced over the intercom. I went down to breakfast and casually dropped a word about this. A gunner captain replied, "Padre, if you are serious about this, I'm sure you wouldn't mind taking a small bet on the subject." While we were discussing this, an announcement came over the ship's P.A. system: we were, indeed, going to join the Eighth Army for an attack on Sicily.

We entered the Mediterranean under cover of darkness. Everyone knew we would be in danger of attack by U-boats and aircraft. The subs hit several ships in our convoy with torpedoes, and we lost the guns of one of our batteries. Survivors struggled to swim in water heavy with oil. This made a number of soldiers very sick. I was told one of them just said, "Oh, what the hell," and slipped under. I believe he was the only casualty of our regiment.

My army kit had been put on one ship and I on another.

I never did find out whether it was I, or my kit, that was on the wrong ship. In any case, I lived, and my kit went to the bottom of the Mediterranean.

For safety's sake, I had duplicated most of my kit and sent it by transport in a large kit bag. It arrived ten days after us, and when I came to the beach to pick it up, I found it had been slashed open with a knife. All that was left in the giant bag were two pairs of woolen long johns and a pair of rubber boots. The temperature was 120 degrees in the shade and I felt like tossing them into the sea. Johnny Westine, my driver, intervened: "Padre, don't throw anything away until January." This proved to be very wise advice, because when January came, and we were in the mud of Ortona, these three items were worth their weight in gold. They were probably worth more than all the things which were stolen.

During our landing, I watched an amusing incident take place. The motor vehicles were all waterproofed. The carburetors had chimneylike air intakes to protect the vehicles so that they could travel in about five or six feet of water. One of these landing craft got stuck on a false beach two hundred yards from the real beach. A jeep left the landing craft and manoeuvred over the sand bar. Unaware that there was deeper water between him and the land, the driver drove into it. Suddenly, his comrades saw his head disappear under water, his hat come to the surface, turn over and sink. Water entered the air intake tube, and the engine choked and stopped. Soon after, the driver came to the surface, cursing, climbed on one of the big lorries which were able to go safety through the deep water, and proceeded ashore.

There weren't any casualties as we approached the beach. But on the beach, death came to one of our soldiers.

The night before we landed on the southeast beach of Sicily, he had told a friend that he felt sure he would be killed the next day. Ten feet from the water's edge, a bullet struck him in the forehead.

That night I lay in a slit trench on the beach and had a very good view of German and Italian bombers flying overhead. We could see the bombs fall from the planes on one side of us, and travel over to land on the other side. I had just rolled over on my stomach when a large piece of flesh fell into my trench and hit me on the back of my neck. At first I thought that I had been hit, and the flesh was my own. It was with relief I verified I was intact and the flesh was not mine. It was a disgusting but happy realization. However, the episode ended my attempts to eat supper.

In the morning I found that a shell-shocked cow had been torn apart by a bomb, and part of her had fallen into my hideout. Perhaps it is hard to believe, but I was grateful when I learned I had been hit by a three-pound raw chunk of bloody beef. The next day we moved inland a little way, and I found myself leaning over a stone fence to pluck ripe grapes from a vine. My companion was a young lieutenant who had joined our regiment in England. As we enjoyed the grapes, our shoulders almost touching, a bullet whizzed between our heads. We both somersaulted over the fence. Lying on our backs, we pulled off grapes and went on eating. Little did I suspect that the young lieutenant, William R. McIntyre, would one day become a Justice of the Supreme Court of Canada.

During our time in Sicily, something happened which caused a significant change in my life. While in England, we had received extensive motorcycle training. I enjoyed these courses, and developed a liking for the Norton motorcycle. It did something for my ego to experience the explosive power of this British machine. Had I been assigned this mode of transport, I would have accepted it willingly. One event, however, changed my mind.

One day in Sicily, I was going uphill rather fast on a motorbike. Coming over the crest, I entered a rock cut. As I did so, the machine travelled a few inches above the ground for twenty feet or so, and I came face to face with a Churchill tank. That in itself would not have posed a problem, except that an Italian woman was meeting the tank, and its noise had drowned out the noise of my machine. She was walking on the outside of the tarmac, less than three feet from the tank. Only five feet separated the woman and the side of the rock cut, and the surface there was covered with five-inch rocks. I hadn't any choice but to go between the woman and the tank – and I had to decide while I was still flying. I squeezed through what seemed to me to be about two feet and, instinctively, pulled in on both handlebars. Once through, I let the machine coast to a stop and topple over, while I lay beside it, drained. Gas and oil dripped from it, and I remember saying to the machine, "Pour away you old beastie."

As I lay there, I thought of all that could have happened. If I had even brushed the tank, it would have thrown me against the woman. If I had hit the woman, I would have careened into the tank which, given my speed, would likely have killed both of us. When the woman came over to me, she asked if I was hurt. I shook my head, and she went on, unaware of how close she had come to dying.

At last I got up, mounted the machine and left it in low gear for the two-mile ride to the regiment. I took it to the headquarters' vehicle park and said to the Staff Sergeant, "Staff, I will not be needing this machine again." I didn't even explain. I travelled with the Medical Officer for a month, until I was able to get a truck. I have never been on a motorcycle since that day.

Sicily is very hot and dry in summer. People there keep water in long, thin, porous jars which they hang from trees. As the water slowly oozes out, evaporation keeps it surprisingly cold, even when the temperature is well over one hundred degrees Fahrenheit in the shade.

Our soldiers were surprised to see many of the Sicilians with flaxen-blonde hair. This was the heritage of Viking pirates who had passed through the land raiding the countries of the Mediterranean.

We noted one phenomenon in Sicily which was strange to us. People returned to their farms after the war in little processions, often passing over unswept mine fields. These were usually families and were arranged as follows: the wife and mother was first in the procession, leading a cow; she would be followed by a group of children; and bringing up the rear would be the husband and father riding a donkey. Our soldiers called it "minesweeping Sicilian style." The Royal Twenty-second Regiment had their own way of attempting to deal with this. I once watched them pull the man off his donkey, put his wife on the beast, then hand him the cow's rope and send him on his way. Of course, as soon as he got out of sight of the soldiers, he would quickly give the rope back to his wife and remount the donkey.

During the Sicilian campaign, we moved forward with the Americans on our left and the British on our right. When we arrived at the town of Adrano, we found it had massive defenses, including reinforced concrete pillboxes. Our field artillery was far too light to be effective against these strong points. Our infantry suffered heavy losses as they tried to storm the boxes. The Air Force was then called in to knock them out. The bomber attack was to be followed by a heavy artillery bombardment, and each gun in the three field regiments had five hundred rounds of ammunition piled beside it.

The air attack was made by four medium bombers. The first three dropped their bombs and eluded the anti-aircraft guns. But the last one had a near miss, which started a fire in one of the engines. Four chutes blossomed out from the stricken aircraft, and we waited anxiously for the fifth to appear. The plane was losing altitude, and I found myself looking directly up the plane's fuselage – it seemed to be heading exactly in my direction. I remember thinking that if it didn't change direction, I would be dead in ten seconds. I also happened to be standing nearly in the centre of the guns which were clustered behind one small hill. This put me in the midst of twelve thousand rounds of live ammunition. There wasn't any place to run.

At the last moment, one wing tilted up, and the plane made a left turn. At this point, the pilot jumped from the plane, but his chute didn't have time to open. He fell several hundred feet to his death. The bomber fell on the kitchen and exploded. The dozen people in the kitchen were so severely burned that they were no longer recognizable to close friends. One of them kept asking for a mirror; another noted that he felt no pain and wondered why; and another asked me how long he would have to stay in hospital.

Throughout the campaign, I had carried twelve self-contained syringes of morphine in the breast pockets of my battledress. I used all of them in a few minutes of that awful day. One of the most severely burned talked steadily as I held his arm with my left hand and gave him two injections of the drug. When I had finished the work and tried to let go, his parched skin stuck to my hand. He didn't notice at all and kept on chattering.

We knew that none of the burned ones had any chance of surviving. All of the nerve endings in their skins were destroyed, and they would all be in shock in a matter of minutes. I felt like a zombie, doing the things I had been taught, making decisions, giving orders, talking quietly as if I had perfect confidence, and knowing all the time that I was working with men who didn't have any chance of recovery. It was a strange experience, and one which underlined the importance of training. I felt as if I were outside my body, giving orders, speaking with a quiet confidence I didn't feel, but grateful to be able to help the stricken ones. We travelled with the casualties until we met the ambulances, and then returned in our lorries to bury the pilot's body.

When it was over, someone played "The Star Spangled Banner" on a trumpet. It was a moving moment. We all knew that in turning the burning plane away from the guns, this brave man had saved the lives of hundreds of our gunners while sacrificing his own. An artillery formation is very different from an infantry unit. Though each of our men had a rifle or a sten gun as his personal weapon, the heart and soul of the artillery regiment were its guns. The American pilot's death stirred our emotions so strongly because he had spared our guns. A young French-Canadian gunner summed it up perfectly, as he looked down on the crumpled form wrapped in an army blanket: "He saved the guns. I'll never call them pigeons again."

The guns and the gunners are a unit. Guns mean little without the gunners, and the gunners are fish out of water without the guns. They lavish extreme care on these instruments of death, as if they were living things. It is almost impossible to explain this relationship to a civilian.

After the war ended, each artillery regiment had a ceremony called 'the resting of the guns'. The whole regiment moved past a reviewing stand where the Brigadier and the Commanding Officer took the general salute. It was a very moving sight. After the march past, the gunners dismounted, and the whole regiment saluted the guns as they were moved away to the gun park. It was like a kind of death and burial.

9

SETTING THE STYLE FOR HOMES
AWAY FROM HOME

My driver, Johnny Westine, was a carpenter and hard rock miner from New Liskeard. He found some lumber and tarp material and managed to transform our 15-CWT truck into a very comfortable caravan. His bed was crosswise right behind the cab, and mine was lengthwise down one side. Attached with hinges to the side of the truck and with steel legs on the inside, it had very comfortable springs. During the day, the beds could be fastened up against the wall. On the other side, there was a small desk with a light powered by a car battery. Above the desk sat a book shelf, and in the back corner, there was a small stove made from an oil drum, which burned a mixture of petrol and kerosene. The fuel could be regulated to drip onto a brick as it burned, so one could have a very low or very high temperature.

Several months after this "van" was completed, the new Regimental Sergeant-Major came to see me. He informed me that it was against regulations for an officer to share quarters with an O.R.(other rank) and suggested that I arrange for Westine to move outside for sleeping.

I rebuffed this suggestion by asking him how we could then move off at two minutes' notice. I asked him again a week later if he had a suggestion, and he replied, "Padre, you know damned well that you are asking the impossible."

"Well," I said, "we can do it nicely with my arrangement, and until you have a workable alternative plan, Sergeant-Major, we will stick to my arrangement."

I expected him to complain to the C.O., and I did have a visit from the Commanding Officer within the week. He took one look and then turned to me.

"Padre, I outrank you. Why should you have better living quarters that I? Might I suggest you lend me your driver for a week? After he builds one for me, you may keep your caravan *and* driver for yourself."

I concurred with a measure of grace, and he got his caravan.

Sometime later on, he was visited by our Divisional Commander, who, upon seeing his caravan, said, "Colonel, I outrank you. Why should you have better quarters than I? I really think you should lend your builder to me for a week so we can right a grievous wrong." Our C.O. found himself in the same spot I had previously occupied, and concurred, likewise, with grace. The General got his caravan. My driver once more cursed under his breath and then, for my benefit, ended up with the English Tommy's pronunciation of a French expression, "Sanferrian – C'est la guerre."

Sicily was what my driver called, "a mixed bag." The air was so dry that if you washed a shirt and hung it up in the wind it would dry in five minutes. Water was scarce but good. Then a rumour started that the Sicilians had poisoned some wells, and we were rationed to one gallon of water per day per soldier. Some of our men, prodigal in drinking the stuff, were reduced to washing their socks in shaving water.

Adrano was a key to the enemy's defence. When it fell they had to evacuate Sicily. Everyone was glad to move closer to Mount Etna – there was a small river flowing down the slopes from the snows of the volcano. We revelled in the luxury of abundant, clear cold water. We even went for a swim in the stream. The only man, though, who could stay in it for more than a few seconds was, strangely enough, a chap from Jamaica.

The fruit trees were in bloom and it was here that I encountered a peculiar plant called 'prickly pear'. Each year at the tip of a cactus stock, there appears a shortened segment. This produces a yellowish flower at its extremity, while the pigment of the plant becomes orange-red. This distinctive plant is expertly cultivated as a fruit by the people. Next to a mango, it is one of the world's most delectable fruits. But it is guarded by the most insidious array of spines in the plant kingdom. When the spines penetrate the skin, they break off and lodge there until they are removed by tweezers or expelled by pus. Most of our men ate only one prickly pear.

One of our despatch riders, though, created an instrument to defeat the P.P. It was a can nailed to a stick. He pushed the can down over the pear, broke off the fruit and nailed it to a board. It could then be dissected with a razor blade, and the pulp safely scooped out. He was not only marked as a genius, but he was the only Canadian to foil the "Sicilian mouse trap." Fortunately for Sicily, we moved across the Reggio Strait before the Canadians could harvest all of the prickly pear crop.

Southern Italy is extremely mountainous. The people are isolated in relatively small communities and are so dissimilar from those of the northern regions that they might be a different people. Throughout Italy they had one thing in common, and that was the main highways. The descendants of the Romans are superb road builders.

The first night we spent in Italy was on one of these beautiful roads. In the mountains the roads have elaborate cement ditches, built to deal with large amounts of water. Our soldiers found the ditches wonderful places to sleep. They had picked up bags of straw in their travels, and they placed these in the smooth waterways and settled down for a good night's sleep. Although we didn't get any rain in our area, the rain did fall higher up, and there was a great hubbub when the water reached us. I looked out of my truck to see mountains of straw, sleeping bags and pieces of army equipment sweeping past. Scantily clad Canadians pulled themselves free of the floating debris, expressing themselves in a most colourful way. They dubbed the event, "Mussolini's revenge," as if the infamy of the flood was due to the treachery of the Duce himself. They were never caught napping again.

Southern Italy was also a land of castles. Many of them were in good repair. These castles fully revealed the character of the southerners, and one in particular was very interesting. It had a large torture room, fitted out with many ingenious devices for causing pain. These included branding irons, a wheel for stretching victims to the breaking point, and an iron boot. The victim's foot would be placed in the boot and the torturer would drive wooden pegs between the boot and the victim's leg – the only possible way to free the victim was to amputate the leg.

Fifteen feet up the wall was a small verandah from

which the lord of the castle could direct the operations. It spoke volumes of the character of the owner who built it. A lady's bedroom also gives another clue about this Lord of the Castle.

There is a story that tells of the owner going on a military mission to another part of Italy. There he heard from a spy that his wife had formed an intimate relationship with his younger brother. In a surprise move, he returned to the castle and proceeded to his wife's boudoir. A guard at the door challenged him and caused a small furor. By the time he gained entrance, his wife was alone in her bed. She protested her innocence, and when he attempted to search her clothes cupboard, she told him that if he did so, he would never receive her love again. He decided not to search the closet. Instead he had two bricklayers brick up the door with a double wall of bricks. When it was done, the lady began a battle of minds with her husband. Each time the husband came to his wife's bedroom, he was greeted with a broad smile. This continued for several years, and he took out his anger and frustration on captured enemies.

Finally one day, when he was riding his horse at full gallop along a narrow mountain trail, the horse stumbled and hurled its master down a steep mountainside to his death. The lady married her husband's cousin and they lived together to a ripe old age. When they died, they took with them the mystery of the new, bearded cousin, whom no one had heard of before.

The old doorkeeper stuck to his story that there wasn't anyone with his mistress on the night her husband stormed up to her bedroom door; the guard on the stairway remained silent.

On the steep mountain roads of the south, we visited

a town called Catanzaro. To get to it, we had to pass through a narrow gorge. It looked as if a great block of gray granite two hundred yards long had been split in two by a giant sword. I didn't see a crack or break in the smooth wall. The jeep had no more than six inches clearance on either side. The sides of the cleft were seventy or eighty feet high. The whole thing looked like the valley of the shadow of death that David speaks of in the shepherd's song.

The people of Catanzaro were typical southerners. As we proceeded up the main street, we passed close to mother pigs feeding their young, chickens, ducks, goats, dogs and cats, mingled with myriads of children. A number of mothers, not at all self-conscious, nursed their children. It was as if the war had hardly touched these ancient people. Our jeep was likely the only war vehicle they had seen, except for planes.

The Canadian Sappers (Engineers) had fun with road signs in this area. They were effective in getting a cautionary message across:

CAN YOUR WIFE REPLACE YOU – IF NOT, CHANGE TO LOW GEAR

WOULD YOU LIKE TO BE A RETURNED SOLDIER – IF SO, SLOWDOWN!

IF YOU SEE THAT GOLDEN STREAM, YOU'VE BEEN TAKING MEPACRINE!

The latter may have been an overflow of sapper exuberance into the Medical Corps.

10

THE SURVIVORS

Every regiment in the Canadian Army during the Second World War had within it at least one very special character who was identified and characterized by the cartoonist, Sergeant Bing Coughlin. Coughlin, the creator of "Herbie" in the army paper *Maple Leaf*, started in Italy on January 14, 1944, and "Herbie" was the life and soul of the paper.

This doughty Canadian soldier was popular with everyone in the army, perhaps because he was so easy to identify with. Each of the cartoons depicted things that had happened in dozens of regiments, dozens of times. The genius of Bing was that he was so close to the life of the army that it was a living, breathing account of our everyday life.

Johnny Westine and I once got ourselves featured in one of Bing's cartoons. One evening, we were slogging through the mud returning to our caravan and I inadvertently stepped in an unmarked shell hole. The universal six inches of mud at Ortona had suddenly become two or three feet, and my efforts to save myself left me sitting in the middle of the shell hole with the thick mud several inches above my waist. There was a deathly silence, and then

Westine, in his inimitable way, said, "Say it, Padre, say it – it's always better to get it out."

Ordinarily, at the end of the day, before entering, I pushed my feet under the end of the caravan, and catching the roof, pulled myself out of my rubber boots. This time, though, after retrieving a very muddy wallet, I unloosened my belt and pulled myself out of my pants.

While we were still stationed in the South of England, our Herbie #1 gained considerable fame for his work in defusing a number of unexploded bombs.

I first met this Herbie in the guard house, where he was under detention for some misdemeanour. I saw that he had received three letters, and commented that I hoped they bore good news. He was silent for a few moments and then answered, "Padre, maybe you could give me an opinion on this. This one here is from my mother – my old man has died. This one is from my sister – she tells me my wife has run away with another man. And this little blue one is from my girlfriend in Yorkshire – she's pregnant." I had to admit that, at the very best, it was a mixed bag.

Now and then, a spell in detention was not an unusual experience for our Herbie. Still, his reputation for defusing unexploded bombs commanded the respect of his peers. One time, he saved a nearby Surrey village from terrible destruction and earned a recommendation for the George Cross.

But shortly after, his adventuresome spirit entangled him in what would have been to anyone else an impossible situation. He was caught, at 2:00 a.m., as an uninvited guest in the darkened downstairs of the home of a retired British Colonel. Herbie, maintaining his usual steely nerve, demanded silence of the Colonel, shushing him in a commanding way, while he mysteriously scanned the room.

Finally, he volunteered to the mystified Colonel: "Well, he's certainly not here. You see, we are looking for a German spy. I was told he might have taken refuge in your house." He then shook hands with the Colonel, bade him goodnight and went on his way.

Shortly after, the local paper printed a picture of our Herbie #1 as the hero who prevented sure destruction by defusing a deeply buried, unexploded bomb in the vicinity. The retired Colonel, having noted this with some astonishment, remarked on meeting our C.O., "By George, Colonel, that gunner of yours is a remarkable chap." He then followed this with an account of his own experience with the 'spy catcher'. Needless to say, when the British Colonel left, the spy catcher was called on the carpet and given twenty-eight days detention.

Unaware of this, the town had organized a reception at which representatives of Whitehall would award Herbie #1 the distinguished George Cross. The town party went on without the chief guest of honour, and Whitehall was not amused to find the recipient in detention. In the end, a medal wasn't ever awarded to Herbie #1.

The British just couldn't bring themselves to bestow an award for bravery to a man in detention.

Herbie #2 was a handsome young French-Canadian who had gone AWOL in 1941. He had returned early the next year to the regiment and given himself up for arrest. He was then court-martialled and sent to the glasshouse for two years. But after only four months of his sentence had been served, his division left for the Mediterranean, and he applied for a "King's Pardon" to join his regiment in battle. Having received the pardon, he duly arrived in

Italy, and it was there I heard his story.

Herbie #2 was a super gambler – he was deadly with a set of dice. I once saw him roll eight winners in succession. While he was AWOL, he had rented a posh flat in the West End of London where he entertained and gambled to his heart's content. As a result of his winnings, he was easily able to afford the high life. He promoted himself to the rank of Captain, all the while keeping a dignified, low profile and being charmingly vague about his job in the military.

Then, a British Captain came to one of his parties and he and Herbie #2 eventually became close friends. After a few months this Captain took Herbie #2 aside, and said, "Captain, I am from Scotland Yard, and I was assigned to investigate you. It was thought you might be a French citizen in the pay of our enemies. I've discovered this is not so, and I have no further professional interest in you. However," he continued, "I have come to admire you. Would you mind awfully if I gave you some advice?"

"Captain," Herbie #2 replied, "I make it a point to take good advice whenever I can."

"Well, my friend, it would appear we will soon have military action; so why not return to your regiment, give yourself up and accept whatever punishment you get in the court martial? Then, when action starts, apply for a King's Pardon in order to fight for your country. This way, you may only serve a fraction of your sentence. You will, of course, receive no pay during the time of your sentence, but I have a feeling this will not be an intolerable burden for you."

Herbie #2 thanked him and took his advice.

He joined us in Italy and was given back his old job but, of course, not his rank. He didn't receive pay for two years. As the British Captain had predicted, this was not a great burden for Herbie. Each payday there was one lineup at the paymaster's vehicle and another at Herbie's truck.

When the war ended, the only way he was able to get his winnings back to Canada was by visiting the big diamond market in Amsterdam and buying a number of large gems. I often wondered if he declared them at Customs when he reached his homeland.

There were countless "Herbies" no less amusing.

One day the C.O. asked me to sit with him while he held court in the orderlies' room. By way of explanation, he said, "Padre, if in the course of events, I appear to be about to commit murder, restrain me. Here's a letter from a woman which will fill you in on the situation." It read:

Dear Colonel, Gunner X spent a seven-day leave with my daughter and me. Since that time we have both discovered that we are pregnant by him. This is a bother, but the real reason for this letter is that he had no money for bus fare when he was returning to the regiment, and he borrowed our bicycle. Would you ask him to return it as soon as possible, as I need it for transport to and from work.

When the case started, the soldier was asked about the bicycle and was given some precise orders in this regard by the C.O.

11

VARIOUS SHADES OF COURAGE

While I served for most of the war with the artillery, I concede that it was the infantry who had everything thrown at them. Rifles, machine guns, artillery of all calibers, mortars, tanks, bombs and land mines – all dealing out an assortment of death to the foot sloggers. Equally as insidious were the enemy's booby traps. There is a story of one infantryman who, coming on a booby trap, attached a stout string to it. Then, taking shelter in a slit trench, he pulled the string. It detonated an explosive in the bottom of the slit trench, killing him.

But all these devices of death were only part of the problem facing those who led men into battle. These leaders first had to strengthen their own resolve before they could lead others. Before they uttered the words, "Lets go," they had to say them to their own bodies in the silence of their own souls. This dichotomy between mind and body is an integral part of deep fear. While I never led men into battle, I became well acquainted with this very insistent emotion. In one severe shelling, when I was with the Second Field Regiment, I heard a man cry out in pain and terror. I remember distinctly thinking to myself that if that last shell had landed five feet away from my trench instead of twenty, it would have broken my ear drums, and I would have been unable to hear the one who called to me – and then I wouldn't have had to go out to help him. The thought lasted only a few seconds but it was very real, as real as it was ugly. Then I said to myself, "Come on, Davey lad, that's one of your men – get out there and do your job!" In a detached way, I saw my legs start to move, carrying me out of that beautiful, safe hole in the ground.

I reached the wounded soldier at the same time as a young captain named Wally Childers. "Padre," he said, "You know –one of us must be crazy." I answered, "It's you, Wally – I have just had the sanest thought you ever heard." We tied up the wounds of the gunner, moved him into a slit trench and made it back to our friendly fox holes without harm.

The following poem, found on the body of an infantry officer named Alex Campbell, of the Hastings & Prince Edward Regiment, gives us valuable insight into the soul of man in this sacred and awful hour.

> *When 'neath the rumble of the guns*
> *I lead my men against the Huns*
> *Tis then I feel so all alone and weak and scared*
> *And oft I wonder how I dared*
> *Accept the task of leading men.*
> *I wonder, worry, fret and then, I pray*
> *Dear God, who promised oft to humble men, to*
> *lend an ear*
> *Now in my troubled state of mind*
> *Draw near O God, draw near, draw near,*
> *Make me more willing to obey*
> *Help me to merit my command.*
> *And if this be my fatal day*

Reach out, O God, Thy helping hand
And lead me down that deep, dark vale.
These men of mine must never know
How much afraid I really am.
Help me to lead then in the fight
So they will say, 'He was a man'.

Similar thoughts were expressed in the following poem. It is a soldier's prayer written on a scrap of paper found fluttering over the desert sands during the battle of El Agheila on December 14th, 1942. The author was never found, and it is presumed that he died in battle.

Stay with me God. The night is dark,
The night is cold; my little spark
Of courage dies. The night is long;
Be with me, God, and make me strong.
I love a game, I love a fight,
I hate the dark; I love the light.
I love my child; I love my wife.
I am no coward, I love life.
I knew that death is but a door.
I knew what we were fighting for;
Peace for the kids, our brothers freed,
A kinder world, a cleaner breed.
I am the son my mother bore.
A simple man, and nothing more.
But – God of strength and gentleness
Be pleased to make me nothing less.
Help me, O God, when death is near
To mock the haggard face of fear,
That when I fall – if fall I must
My soul may triumph in the dust.

I believe that no one can really know himself until he has felt the all-searing heat of the crucible of terror. Before that moment I had tried to prepare myself. I had watched all of the motion pictures of World War I. I had sweated it out in such movies as *All's Quiet on the Western Front.* I had even considered how I would act under fire. Conceding that I would be terrified, I honestly believed that I would move about with quiet efficiency, doing what I had to do.

The moment of truth arrived with five enemy shells landing in as many seconds, killing or wounding eight of our comrades. Right away I knew I was in a different world. I heard a tough soldier cry out in pain and terror, begging a close friend to staunch his wounds, some of which were spurting bright red blood. He spoke to his friend: "Bill, if you save my life, I will be your slave forever." In no time at all, a naked, bloody-awful terror stripped us clean of all theatrics, all play acting, all heroic little plans. As terror preyed on our survival instincts, lesser things were swept away. Even bravery took on a vastly different form. It took an immense effort to do even the obvious and ordinary. Without the least surprise, we would watch a brave soldier dive into a filthy, shallow cesspool to escape the clawing fingers of death. In a few seconds, that shocking crescendo of living hell taught me more about myself than all the movies, all the books of war, all the lectures and all the studied plans of the army manual, put together.

Some men show an incredible coolness under fire. Slim Babkirk came from the Peace River country. I believe he was about eighteen years old when he joined the regiment. He was well over six feet tall, with an angular body which he moved with graceful ease. He spoke with a western drawl with a tinge of John Wayne about it.

Slim's job was to protect his battery against enemy patrols and fighter planes. His weapon was a Bren gun. The weapon weighed twenty-two pounds, but Slim used it like a tommy gun. I had been impressed when the instructor at Bordon, Hants, told us to hold it close to our shoulders; otherwise, it could break a collar bone. We fired it lying down, its muzzle resting on a bipod.

One day, near the East Coast of Italy, I was talking to Slim as he ate a corned beef sandwich. As he ate, he balanced the Bren on the inside of his thigh with his left hand. Suddenly, he dropped the sandwich on the damp earth, grasping the trigger area with his right hand. Three Messerschmits came in low over the treetops a few hundred yards away. Before their guns opened fire, Slim Babkirk's Bren roared into action and arched his fire into the belly of the enemy machine. We saw the bullets hit. The plane climbed suddenly at a steep angle away from the formation and then fell in a blaze of smoke and flame into the sea. As the wounded machine began it precipitous climb, Slim drawled, "Gotcha, Fritzi."

But some men who volunteered for active service found they had no capacity whatsoever to face enemy fire. There was a regimental M.O. who, during the Sicilian Campaign, acknowledged his fear openly. He operated out of a deep slit trench, and he refused point-blank to move out of it. With each position, he dug a new trench. His fear was affecting the troops, and the C.O. asked me to talk to him. Our discussion was brutally frank. He said he was terrified, wanted to be moved out of the front line, and he didn't much care how it was done.

I went to the Second in Command of the regiment and got him to promise that if the M.O. applied for a transfer, he would support it, and that it would be done quietly, without malice or reproach. Unfortunately, once the process started, it quickly moved out of control. To this day, I think our Adjutant was honest about the procedure; it was simply taken out of his hands by the higher authorities. The latter were logical and just, asking why an officer should be given special treatment. They were right in one way and wrong in another. The army lost an excellent surgeon, one who could have been used to good effect in a base hospital, because the book said such officers should be court-martialled and put out of the army.

The truth was that everyone was scared at the front. Training and discipline will help most soldiers to carry out their duties in spite of their fears, but it doesn't alter the fact that everyone in their right mind is scared when bullets and shell fragments are flying and bombs and mines are exploding. Although some acted nonchalant, the battle-wise soldier knew that eventually the piper would have to be paid.

The new M.O. was a heavyset, six-foot man. Originally he came from the Maritimes, but he had worked in a hospital in Southampton, England, for several years before the war broke out. When I went to him, he looked at me quizzically and then said with a warm smile, "Padre, I am wondering how you and I will get along. You see, I'm an atheist and a dialectic materialist. It would seem difficult for us to live on the same street, let alone find an easy way to talk about anything but the weather."

I replied that I got along fairly well with my last Bishop, and refused to rule out the possibility of success with him.

At this he laughed loudly, "I like that! You know, Padre. We just might be able to pull it off."

As it turned out, we became close friends, and while we were diametrically opposed on some subjects, we were very close indeed on many others. On one occasion, we found ourselves isolated and opposed by those in command of the affairs of the regiment.

The army setup kept us close together in the field. We talked long and loud on many subjects. I found him to be a master debater, but surprisingly fair. One day, he expressed puzzlement. "Padre, you obviously believe in evolution. How do you accommodate this with the teaching of your church as defined by Bishop Ussher?" (This cleric had worked out a timetable of creation covering about four thousand years, which I personally had rejected before I left high school.)

For his edification, I gave him a Bible with the Genesis account of creation, admonishing him to remember that the Bible says one thousand years in God's sight is like the difference between the end of one hour and the beginning of the next.

When he finished reading, he said, "While I still do not agree with your premise, it is the best I have ever read, and it does pose a relevant question. How could the writer of this account have known that life began in the sea, and from that base populated the whole earth?"

In one area in Central Italy, the enemy decided that defence would be difficult and made a twenty or thirty mile retreat in record time. We were travelling along quickly, and still we didn't make contact with the enemy. One night, we camped in open country without slit trenches and gun pits. Suddenly, the enemy air force dropped magnesium flares, and their fighters were able to strafe us at low level. When this happened, I was in the

R.A.P.(Regimental Aid Post) tent with the M.O. The flares made us stand out like a sore thumb, and without slit trenches we felt very naked. We did the only thing we could do – we lay on our backs, looking up at the brilliant sky.

Some of our men crawled under their vehicles for protection, only to have the bullets pierce their gas tanks, spray them with gasoline and set them on fire. At one point, we saw several men running around like torches.

We noted that the planes were making their runs from north to south, probably in order to avoid collisions. I distinctly remember thinking that the south side of a big tree would be safer than lying on a tarp beside this dialectic materialist. A stubborn pride kept me from moving to what I knew would be a saner position.

After they had made two strafing passes thirty-odd feet on either side of us, I heard the M.O.'s careful drawl, "Padre, if I'm killed tonight, will you give me a Christian burial – and if so, why?"

I knew that most of his questions were loaded, so I carefully thought the matter over for what seemed an interminable length of time. Finally, I answered him. "Yes, Mo, I would, and do you know why? There was a certain man who had two sons. The old man asked them to help him on the farm. The first agreed, but he went to sleep under a tree. The second son told his father what he could do with the job and walked off. Then he thought it over and changed his mind. He came back and worked all day. Mo, do you recognize yourself?"

I knew I had scored.

As we attended to the wounds and burns of our casualties we heard our own guns strike back. A parachute came down close by. This ended the strafing, much to our relief. I went over to where the parachute had fallen and found a very frightened German pilot surrounded by a grim ring of angry gunners. The pilot was unarmed and terrified – and with good reason. One of the gunners was holding a bayonet under his chin and screaming, "You killed my best friend, you f.....ing bastard."

When I stepped into that circle, my sympathies were totally with the gunners. Nevertheless, I found myself playing devil's advocate for the prisoner.

"Fellows, you can't kill this prisoner. The intelligence boys need him for questioning."

I knew that what I was saying was nonsense – I didn't care a damn about the intelligence boys, and part of me would have rejoiced if the prisoner's parachute had failed to open.

But the next day my decision was affirmed when a group of the gunners came to me and said, "You were right, Padre, it would have been wrong to kill him." Even the M.O. chuckled that morning, saying, "Padre, for a fellow who is totally wrong, you do come up with some big winners." Even in war, it is wrong to take the life of another human being.

Some time later, when we were taken out of the line after sustaining heavy casualties, the incidence of V.D. went up about one thousand percent. Some of our senior officers, in their wisdom, decided to start a brothel. In this way, they believed they could strictly control, and thereby guard, the health of the regiment.

I heard this news on the grapevine and, being miffed that they were acting behind my back, was seized with outrage. In righteous fury, I called a regimental church parade for Sunday, and there I told the regiment to disregard the moral leadership of their senior officers.

One of those senior officers came to see me after the service and said, "My God, Padre, why did you do that? You reprimanded the C.O. and all four Majors of the regiment in front of the whole parade. I don't know what they will do to you. This has never happened before. The rule book certainly doesn't cover it, but I know something has to happen. Why did you do it? Why didn't you come to us and tell us by ourselves?"

That officer may have been right. It probably would have been far better to call them to a private conference. But I was afraid I would be told to mind my own business.

After the parade, on my way back to my caravan, I looked in on the M.O. at the Regimental Aid Post. Having heard the news before I arrived, he looked at me quizzically and drawled, "Padre, you are a fool. You realize, of course, that you and I will be kicked out of the regiment tomorrow."

"What do you mean, we? You weren't even at church parade," I answered.

"Padre," he replied, "for the first time in my life I am truly sorry I missed a church parade. Nevertheless, you are a fool, Padre. You and I will be kicked out of the regiment and we will remain captains for the duration of the war. Oh yes, I forgot to tell you – I gave the boys a bit of a going over last night too, so we will be kicked out together, and by Christian officers. Life is strange, isn't it?"

At this point the M.O. was called away by a runner, and I had to get the story from his Sergeant, Ace Mitton, who told me word for word what happened:

"The four Majors trooped into our tent and asked the M.O. for an interview. They said they were worried about the jump in the incidence of V.D. in the regiment and decided to do something about it. So they contracted with some Italian girls to co-operate in an effort to create a brothel. They were to be well paid, and all of them were volunteers. They would be checked daily by the M.O. for disease in the hopes that with a controlled brothel they would be able to cut out V.D. in the regiment in a few months."

To this the M.O. had replied, "Gentlemen, if I may call you gentlemen, I don't think I have ever met more disreputable and degenerate characters than you. I won't condemn you for ignorance of things medical. To be fair, while you were learning to sell bonds or run an insurance company, or whatever, I was learning medicine. But I want you to realize that your plan could never work.

"The majority of men who contract V.D., do so when they are inebriated. Soldiers will continue to pick up women on the street, become infected and then come to your brothel and infect some of the inmates. Then a man who thinks he's protected will have a good chance of becoming infected.

"I would also like to know how you can justify taking the lives of fifteen people of another nation and destroy them, for a very questionable purpose. Perhaps, gentlemen, you could explain that, at least to me."

The Sergeant continued, "They got up one at a time; and beginning with the eldest, they filed out of the room into the night."

Later that day I met up with the M.O. I said to him, "Every day I've heard you say: 'Religion is the opiate of the masses. God is dead, Padre. Your religion is an unreality; it's not connected to real life.' And yet, Mo, I find you walking closer to God's will than anyone I know, including myself.

"Yesterday you endangered your army career – insured you will never be promoted – and for what? To save and protect fifteen Italian prostitutes from exploitation. Now, my friend, one question for you – if, as your dialectic-materialism theory maintains, these people are only poor specimens of female primate mammals, why on earth did you risk your future to save them?"

The M.O. chuckled to himself and drawled, "Go to hell, Padre."

I knew I had scored again.

Two days later he was moved by the Medical Corps to a serving hospital. His surgical skills were not being fully utilized in a regiment; but, on the other hand, it was sad and unjust that he was pushed out of the regiment.

My senior padre called me in and told me he had been informed of what had happened. When he heard what I had done, he admitted I might have handled it differently, but he told the regimental authorities that if I had not done what I did, he would have fired me himself. Furthermore, he told them that if I wanted to be moved, he would move me; otherwise, I could stay.

I stayed, though it was somewhat painful. The only table conversation I had for a month or so was to the extent of, "Please pass the mustard."

It is true, time heals all wounds, and it did so in our mess. I thought of apologizing to all concerned, but to do so I would have had to differentiate between one and another. I finally decided it was best to express my regrets to the C.O. and leave the rest of the matter where it belonged – in the past.

As soon as Captain Woolner left the regiment, we received an M.O. who had hair the colour of fire. He seemed utterly oblivious to danger, sitting on a chair and eating his supper while all hell was breaking loose around him. I was slightly embarrassed after I returned to the table for the second time in half an hour to hear him say, "Padre, those fellows couldn't hit the broad side of a barn." I remained unconvinced.

Needless to say, this red-headed Irish-Canadian was popular with the troops. He cajoled the malingers, he strengthened the weak, and he encouraged the frightened. He also had a tremendous wit. In fact, he was a great asset to the regiment.

He was also popular in the mess for having received the largest bottles of wine. This was the result of his having treated some people of an Italian village. One bottle held, I believe, in excess of five gallons, and he donated it to the mess.

But then, little by little, he began to drink to excess. Finally one day, he failed to appear for medical parade. The Adjutant came to me and said, "Padre, the M.O. is drinking and carrying two hand guns. The C.O. thinks we will have to arrest him and send him out. If I do this, though, he will be court-martialled and cashiered. But if you could get his guns away from him, we could just send him out as a medical casualty. In this case, I can guarantee he wouldn't be cashiered."

We were, at the time, billeted in a small Italian town, well away from the firing line. I set out to visit the M.O. and soon met him on the street. When I saw him I thought of Wordsworth's phrase, "a lovely apparition sent to be a moment's ornament," for there he was, in all his glory, walking down the centre of the street like John Wayne. He was wearing only an officer's forage cap, a two-holster gunbelt with two forty-five calibre pistols, and a pair of officer's boots, unlaced. This was his uniform.

Stopping fifty feet from me and drawing both pistols, he said, "Padre, stand a little to the left – my guns shoot to the right."

For want of something better to say, I commented, "Hi, Mo! If you're going to shoot me, shouldn't you first buy me a drink?"

To this, he replied, "How remiss of me, Padre. Come with me, I know a publican who can hardly wait to serve us."

He took me to a small wine shop, which emptied quickly as we approached. The vendor looked as if he would have liked to disappear with his customers, but he was too late. The M.O. called a greeting to him, ushering him back into the now empty shop. He explained to the publican what he wanted, in pidgin Italian. When the latter failed to understand his attempt at Italian, he drew one of his pistols and shot a bottle on the top shelf, remarking, "The one to the left of that one is the one I want."

As the doctor unloosed his gunbelt and laid it on the table beside him, I toyed with the idea of snatching the belt away from him. But he just smiled and said, "Don't even think of it, Padre!"

I didn't consider it again either.

He drank steadily for about an hour. Then, as he talked about home and family, he became very sentimental, and at length he told me how scared he was. It was the first time he had ever even spoken about fear, and it spilled out like a gushing stream. Finally he put his hand on his gunbelt and pushed it over to me.

"You might as well take those bloody things, Padre. I have no more use for them."

We went back to his billet, and he shaved and freshened up. Putting on a fresh uniform, he helped his batman pack his kit and then went quietly to the regimental office. The Adjutant was to go with him to Division Headquarters, where it was arranged for him to go to be booked into a base hospital.

When we were saying goodbye, he looked at me and said, "You're a funny old stick, Padre." And then, in a lower tone, he added, "Thanks a lot."

I never saw him again, but I will remember his gentleness and his caring. He was an excellent doctor.

Fear affects mankind in many different ways. Some retreat to army manuals, sticking to regulations as if they were the law of Medes and the Persians. One Regimental Sergeant-Major insisted on having inspections on parade, even when we were being shelled. Once, when we were getting ready to bury the body of a soldier, the enemy suddenly began to drop a number of random shells on us. The Regimental Sergeant-Major had organized a burial party at the same time we had to take cover from the shelling.

This being one of our first casualties, the party had dug a rather big grave. It was seven feet long, five feet wide and four feet deep. We had just lowered the body into the grave when we heard the enemy guns and knew we had only seconds to react. Without a word, all of us hopped down into the grave. Some of the shells came very close, and as we huddled beside the body, one of the boys whispered to the corpse, "Sorry to crowd you, Herb old cock, but it's awful rough up there, and we're trying to cheat the R.S.M. out of having us dig another grave. You know, he nearly got us all killed digging yours."

As we waited for the shelling to stop, the R.S.M. came

to me and said, "Padre, we mustn't let the enemy think we are afraid to carry out our duties during a shelling."

I replied, "Sergeant-Major, the book also says, 'At no time should a soldier needlessly expose himself to enemy fire.' We will call the burial party when the shelling stops."

It was some time later that the R.S.M. retired and was sent back to Canada. It was a blessed event, though. People who cannot deviate from the book are always a menace to life and limb. However, to do this fine permanent force man justice, I never saw him show any fear. In fact, he was the only soldier I ever saw of whom I could say that.

12

WHO MINISTERS TO
A PADRE IN BATTLE?

At the Hitler line in central Italy, we suffered very severe casualties. It was not easy to fit raw reinforcements into a regiment which had been together since the outbreak of war. New men were at a disadvantage, particularly when they were thrown into battle with veterans of the action. This is just what happened during the battle of Assoro Ridge. The guns so decimated a crack enemy regiment that they were forced to leave the town virtually in the control of an assault company of the Hastings & Prince Edward Regiment. But, as usual, our biggest problems came when we were in a rest area and away from the front.

At this time, I had a long talk with our Medical Officer. He told me that a new strain of V.D. had appeared at one of our base hospitals and was totally resistent to our finest drugs. He concluded frankly, "This might mean that some of our soldiers will be hospitalized for the duration unless we find a new treatment."

One of the reinforcements was a very earnest young man of eighteen, who was trying very hard to grow up and gain the approval of his new comrades. However, some of those comrades needed watching, so I went to look him up. It soon became clear that two friends had already decided to take charge of his 'growing up' and had given him some questionable advice. They had told him to first get drunk on Vino Rosso and then visit an institution called Sister Sophia's Rest Rooms. I learned this when I overheard a conversation between two gunners.

I went straight to the two characters concerned and said, "Listen, you two clutzes, when are you going to start using your heads for something other than a post to hang your tin hats on?" I then acquainted them with my conversation with the M.O. and went on to suggest that they just might make it impossible for the kid to get back to his family at the end of the war.

They were very quiet when I suggested someone should go and get him out of Sophia's place. So, in a pique, I said, "All right, you bastards, if you haven't the guts to go after him, I'll do it myself. I knew then this was not a fair statement, but I wasn't feeling particularly big-hearted at that moment. I left them and went out of the room, closing the door not too gently behind me.

As I walked down the street, I started to cool off, and I felt very much alone. This feeling grew considerably as I approached Sophia's place. I had heard she had broken a chair over some steel helmets a few days earlier. As I drew near the big verandah, I became more and more unsure, but not so unsure that I was ready to give up the project. The proverb came to mind 'Fools rush in where angels fear to tread.' When I was only a few feet away from the place, I heard the scuffle of army boots on the sidewalk behind me, and the two soldiers caught up with me. I could have hugged them.

One of them put his arm around my shoulder and said, "Padre, if I was in Sister Sophia's place, I wouldn't want you to find me there. Let Bill and I get little Bo Peep out and bring him to you."

I replied rather coldly, "You fellows are all heart." But I let them go.

They brought their Bo Peep not to me, but to the M.O., which was what I would have done in any case.

Bill, who was a bit of a joker, said, "I told Fred we couldn't fool you, Padre. We might as well admit that our real fear was you might give the regiment a bad name. Think how humiliated we would feel if it came out in the *Maple Leaf*, under a big headline: Third Field Padre kicked out of Sophia's cathouse with a black eye?"

I'm glad I had the good grace to laugh, thank them both and gratefully return to my billet.

A couple of days later, Sister Sophia came up behind me on the street and said, "Parocchio, not to worry about your Bo Peepo. He pass out on Vino Rosso and I put him in my own bed for safe keeping. But I charge your two bastards full price for him. Not to worry, Parocchio, about Bo Peepo."

Once when I was talking to a bunch of peacetime Chaplains, one of them asked, "Who ministers to the padre in battle?"

I replied, "Once when I needed most to be ministered to, the job was done by two of the roughest, toughest gunners I ever knew, and by an Italian Madame who previously had broken a chair over their heads."

13

A PROPOSAL OF MARRIAGE

We had one memorable visit to Rome. My sister, Eva, had sent me a copy of *The Robe*, and I read most of it while sitting on one of the hard stone seats which were interspersed throughout the Piazza Del Populo. From there, one can see most of ancient Rome, as well as the yellow Tiber River where so much of the story took place. Some of the time I walked up and down the square.

When I am reading a book, I am quite oblivious to what goes on around me. After a while that day, I became vaguely aware that someone had sat down close beside me. I was already sitting at the end of the bench and so couldn't move any farther. I then became aware that a man had stopped and was standing directly in front of me. Looking up I saw a tall American soldier. Bending towards me, he said in a terse whisper, "Bud, de young lady is trying to give you de glad eye."

Looking around, I found that the person sitting so close beside me was indeed young and very beautiful. The whole thing seemed so funny, I couldn't resist laughing. This must have seemed rude because the lovely lady got up quickly and walked away. The American just stood and looked at me as if I were crazy. He stayed for a while shaking his head slowly from side to side, then said, "Geeze," and walked away.

There is a strange ending to this story. I awakened from my long reverie with my book and found, after sitting so long, I was stiff and sore and cold in places. I put the book down and decided to take a short walk. When I turned around to walk back to the bench, the book was gone, and there wasn't anyone near the bench. By now I was definitely not laughing. I still had some of the book left to finish.

Still, the episode did lead to a delightful interlude with a charming Roman family in their home. When I accosted the only people in the square – a man and woman and a small child – and asked them if they'd seen my book, I discovered they spoke English. And they were so sympathetic about my loss that they extended an invitation to my driver and me to spend the next two nights with them. Westine, concerned about the possibility of finding some parts of the caravan missing in the morning, chose to sleep there instead.

The couple had a little six-year-old daughter, who was very open and friendly. She was curious about Canada, so her mother showed it to her in an atlas. She also asked lots of questions. Her parents were highly amused when she suggested they keep me at their house until she was old enough to marry me. It was the first and only marriage proposal I ever received.

John Westine told me that several times during the night he had had to chase people away who had taken a shine to his hubcaps. This inclination to collect things was not so much a lack of moral integrity, as it was a product of extreme poverty. During the time that they were occupied by the German Army, something to barter, including the services of a female member of the family, often made the difference between being hungry and starving. And, to a large extent, this process was maintained after the allied troops overran the towns and villages. It was sad to see attractive female members listed as a course in a menu for a meal served in a private home on some side street. Even middle-class families, desperate to earn their own food and perhaps restore the family finances, resorted to this end.

One such menu earned the boy, who was displaying it to passersby, a clout in the ear by a priest walking with me. The menu for a meal costing "5 dollar" was:

Pasta
Salade
Biftek
Patata Frit
Signorina
Vino Rosso

Hunger is a hard master!

Two fellow officers of the Third Field also made this discovery on a seventy-two-hour leave in Naples. When they entered the city, a small boy jumped on the running board and said, "Maple Leaf Club, Signor – I get you there through thick and thin."

After a long route through the old part of the city, they finally arrived at the Maple Leaf Club. The boy asked them to stop before they entered the MLC compound because, he said, civilians couldn't go there. The officers were feeling generous and each of them gave him a big tip. The boy went on his way. But as they entered the Club property, they realized that all their kit was missing. They had no alternative. They called the regiment and had some new essential kit sent up – including razors. To say this invited a bit of ribbing is an understatement. It was clear now why their guide had wanted to stop outside the compound. It was also clear what had happened in the narrow streets of Old Naples where they had driven slowly enough for nimble urchins to crawl into the back of the vehicle and toss their gear into ever-helpful hands.

14

THE POWER OF PAPER

It was called the paper war. Paper forms, requisitions, moving orders – they were as necessary to a soldier as the air he breathed and the food he ate. (That, too, was obtained with a requisition form duly stamped and signed with illegible signatures.)

Company clerks were the only people who could comprehend the multiplicity of papers. It was the clerk who found the right form, found the correct rubber stamp, and obtained from the C.O., the Adjutant, or the R.S.M., the illegible signatures.

While I was looking for a gunner who had done something illegal, I came across a company clerk who had committed the almost perfect crime. He knew every form used in the army. He had managed to collect and load thousands of the forms and then rubber stamp them in an abandoned vehicle. Thereafter, he recruited some helpers and went AWOL.

After requisitioning a small Italian hamlet, he moved in, pushing his hosts into rather cramped quarters. Next, he requisitioned a typewriter (using a proper form, stamped with a proper stamp). From this base he built his empire, drawing rations and supplies for a number of fictitious soldiers, and subsequently selling them on the black market. He had learned the numbers of all the units and invented a new one for himself. He had a driver – in fact, he made it a point never to drive himself. The civilians, among whom he lived, were very grateful for his largess, and they granted him some very special privileges in return. Fitted out with a Colonel's uniform, every part of it official and perfect, he seemed destined to be set up until the end of the war.

Then he broke three of his own rules. First, he drove his staff car into Rome and allowed himself to be persuaded by an American Colonel to go to a bar. There he was given a drink which he later described as a "time bomb." He then took a second drink – breaking rule number two. Finally, he left the bar and walked to his staff car which was parked directly in front of a Provost Office.

When he got out in the fresh air, the second 'time bomb' went off and he knew he was in trouble. He was barely able to make it to the car, and when he took out his key, he inserted it in the lock upside down. In haste, he tried to force the key and bent it out of shape. A Provost Corporal came out and offered to have the key straightened by an expert. He was having this done when a Captain enquiried as to the number of the vehicle. This started a chain of inquiry that eventually led to the clerk's exposure.

However, this lowly clerk did prove that the man who has all the right forms, and knows how to use them, is a very powerful individual.

15

JOHNNY WESTINE

One day when my driver, Johnny Westine, and I were converging on our vehicle from different directions, he was struck in the arm by a sniper's bullet. It was a flesh wound, and he was back from hospital in a few weeks. But Captain Woolner, our erstwhile famous agnostic M.O., had been greatly amused by the fact that Westine was hit and not me; and, in his famous drawl, he had said, "That's what you get when you have a driver who looks like a padre, and a padre that looks like a driver." This, of course amused Johnny very much.

Johnny had a wonderful sense of humour. He was always regaling me with the latest humorous incident. One of his favorites was the legendary response one of our gunners gave to questions from Colonel Ralston, Minister of National Defence, when he was visiting the troops in Italy.

All VIPs like to shake hands, and this man was no exception. He approached a group of gunners, and putting out his hand to one of them, he said, "Son, what would you like to be when the war is over?"

Quick as a flash, that servant of the guns replied, "A

returned soldier, sir."

Undaunted by this reply, the great man pursued the question, "Being a gunner, I suppose you would be on the lookout for the shell with your name on it?"

"No, sir, actually the one that scares hell out of me is the one with 'For whom it may concern' on it."

Westine was also superb at "scrounging." This was a time-honored institution in the army that included trading soap, bully beef, egg powder and dehydrated mutton with the civilian population for things such a bread, pasta, tomatoes, tomato paste, eggs and Italian ham, as well as the staple drink of Italy – Vino Rosso.

While scrounging was officially illegal, it was a means of widening the variety of everyday food by men fed up with the monotony of plain army rations. I have always liked corned beef, but many soldiers got so fed up with it that they traded it with American troops for Spam. In this transaction, they would often get two or three tins of Spam for one of bully beef. When we moved north in Italy, the boys often got good deals trading the bully beef for eggs, tomatoes and bread.

One time, tired of hardtack biscuits, I was determined to buy a loaf of Italian bread. When we made a convoy stop in a village, I saw two young Italian matrons baking bread in an outside oven, and I started bargaining for one of the big wheel-like loaves. I offered one dollar for the loaf, but when they appeared hesitant, I raised it to two dollars – then three. Finally, seeing that we were about to move on, I raised the ante to four dollars, saying, "You people are too greedy – here's your money, and I'm taking the biggest loaf."

I believe it was the thought of eating the treacherous hardtack, which often splintered and stabbed the roof of my mouth, that prompted me to pay far more than the going price. As I picked up the bread, one woman said to the other, "My God, I think it really is the bread he wants after all."

I suddenly realized that there was definitely a misunderstanding, just as Westine arrived back. As the women dissolved into hilarious laughter, he added, "I think it might be wise to let me look after our commercial interests. This is a wicked, wicked world, Padre."

As I tossed him the great loaf, I conceded that he was probably right. But that night, as we made our evening meal of the best loaf of bread I'd ever tasted, I admitted to Westine that if they had held out, I might have even offered our spare tire as a last resort.

One of our gunners didn't fare as well. He went to a town in the mountains with a bunch of secondhand boots, a box of soap, ten tins of bully beef and a tin of egg powder. For this, he received mounds of bread, eggs, pasta, tomato paste and a demijohn of vino. Just when he was ready to return, an Italian arrived with a ham and a wad of money, wanting a pair of boots and five gallons of gas. The young trader thought for a moment, then whipped off his boots, siphoned five gallons of gas from his jeep and finished the deal. Then he started back to the regiment.

Unfortunately, he ran out of gas half a mile from our lines and hid his loot in a small cave. He set out for the regiment in his sock feet. Ordinarily, he could have made it back, but two Canadian provosts caught up with him and didn't buy his story. He was brought back to the regiment and handed over to the Adjutant, who severely reprimanded him and duly charged him for the loss of his boots. Suspecting he'd sold the gas tank dry, the Adjutant sat him down and told him the fable of the greedy dog.

Later, he was allowed to go and retrieve his cache.

Westine and I had a unique relationship. He was, by the nature of things, a part of regimental headquarters and, therefore, on paper, under the authority of the R.S.M. On the other hand, as I sometimes served the three artillery regiments of the First Division, and he was my driver, he attended very few headquarters' parades. When a parade was called, he often discovered that he needed to take our vehicle to have something repaired at L.A.D. (Light Aid Detachment), permanently attached to the Third Field to handle serious vehicle repairs.

Although he managed to miss almost every parade, he did things for me which were far beyond the call of duty. He helped me take information from the pockets of enemy dead, and at places like Leon Forte that was a messy business – twenty-five bodies had lain in the sun for three or four days. Once, we had to bury nearly fifty putrefying bodies with the aid of a bulldozer. We sent the personal effects of these enemy soldiers, such as letters and photos, to the Red Cross. Often we would see pictures of handsome young soldiers, which bore no resemblance to the grotesque forms of the dead.

Of course, we had to collect information on our own dead, as well, and forward it to Army Headquarters; but nearly all of these men were buried the same day that they fell. One day, we were doing this for an infantryman of the Hastings & Prince Edward Regiment. Westine was resting his writing pad on the limb of an olive tree as I read out the information to him. Suddenly, a bullet whizzed past his head, cutting off a leaf which fell at his feet. I suggested it might be a good idea if he got down beside me with his pad flat on the ground. Johnny answered, "Padre, I have a better idea – let's get the hell outa here." I let myself be persuaded.

One day, a gunner named "Pinky" was killed. We buried him in a rather miserable grave in rain-soaked soil. Some time after midnight, a gunner rapped on our caravan door. I turned our lights out and opened the door. It was a gunner from Pinky's battery, and he asked if he could talk to me. Invited in, he sat on the side of my bed, while I sat at my desk. When the door was shut and we had turned the lights on, we saw that he was a veritable mud-ball. He had evidently tripped and fallen into a mud-filled shell hole. I heard Johnny curse under his breath as he turned his back on the depressing sight.

The soldier wasted no time. "Padre," he began, "You may not know it, but I'm as drunk as a skunk. After the funeral today I felt so low that I hit the bottle. You see, Padre, Pinky and I were very close. In 1932 we left home because our families could no longer support us. We were only thirteen years old. We did odd jobs, and when one of us had work we both ate. Sometimes we didn't eat too well. When the war started, we joined the army and we've been together right up to today, closer than brothers. Now today at the funeral you said, 'If a man die, shall he live again?' You know, Padre, that's the sixty-four dollar question. If I was really sure of that – if I was sure I'd meet Pinky again – I'd be able to cope with saying good-bye to him. Now tell me, Padre, if a man dies, will he live again?"

Replying out of that sad quagmire of mud and filth and death, I said, "Son, there are not too many things we can be certain of in this life, and I've had my share of uncertainties, but I can tell you this – I bank my whole life on the premise that if a man dies, he will live again. I believe with all my heart that we will see Pinky again."

He got unsteadily to his feet, "That's good enough for

me. Good night, Padre."

I turned off the light and opened the door, warning him about the long way down. He stepped out into the night and promptly fell flat on his face in the mud. Getting up again, he said, "That's a real long step down... But I'll be all right – I feel better now. Good night, Padre," and off he went into the dreary, wet night.

When I turned around and put the light on, I found Johnny scraping the thick mud off the canvas cover of my sleeping bag with a table knife and putting it in a tin can. Then he slid into his sleeping bag and, after a few minutes, thought out loud, "I've often wondered about that myself... Good night, Padre." And he was asleep in five minutes.

The next day the C.O. asked me to go to the base hospital and bring him a report on our wounded. I left in half an hour, travelling about fifty miles. We parked our caravan on a cobblestone square beside a spring in a small Italian hamlet. It was good to get away from the mud and the constant shelling. It was very windy and we thought it unsafe to light the stove in our caravan. But when Johnny lit a Primus stove and attempted to cook outside, the wind blew the flame out. After he'd tried three times, an Italian woman came and offered to cook our supper inside her home. Westine was so pleased that he gave her supplies for the entire family, including a whole pound of Maxwell House coffee, telling her to make coffee for her family as well. She cooked a fine meal, adding beautiful Italian bread and pan-fried potatoes as a surprise. When the coffee came, we found she had put nearly one pound of coffee into our eight-cup pot. The brew was impressive to say the least, and even when liberally laced with condensed milk, was almost too much for two Canadians.

We could hardly complain, however, when after supper she took away our dishes and the depleted coffee pot and returned them spotlessly clean. After she left, Westine grumbled, "These Italians are not too bright, you know."

Next morning I looked out to see the lady of the house spreading the coffee grounds out on sheets of newspaper to dry in the bright sunshine. I muttered, "You're right, Westine – these Italians are not too bright."

He was up in a flash and, looking out, expostulated, "Those damned crooks."

I reminded him that we had two and a half pounds of coffee in reserve – in other words, we were stinking rich. He cooled off quickly, muttering to himself, as was his wont.

We visited two base hospitals where we found all our wounded. Coming around a corner of the hospital, I couldn't avoid a head-on collision with a Canadian nursing sister. She was the first Canadian girl I had seen since we arrived in the Mediterranean area, and she was unbelievably beautiful. I tried to apologize, but my mouth wouldn't work. All I could muster was something between a grin and a stunned smile. The young lady was very understanding. She told me she was on her way for a coffee break, and asked me to join her in the mess tent. By that time, I had got my tongue back and accepted her gracious invitation. The episode underlined the obscene reality of the life we were leading in the mudhole called Ortona.

On the return journey, we passed through a small town on the Adriatic coast, where we saw a restaurant with a sign reading, "Biftek, pasta, chips, etc." 'Biftek' was the Italian effort at the words beef steak. Pulling up, we went inside and sat at the first free table we saw. Almost immediately, I was approached by an officer of a British Commando Unit (I believe he thought he should rescue me from having to dine with an O.R.) He invited me to join him and a fellow officer, while one of his O.R.s invited Johnny to join them. It was all quite cozy.

When my order arrived I was surprised at how generous and tasty it was and remarked that I would never again distrust 'biftek'. My commando friend thought he should warn me that it was not really beef steak but "young mule." I replied, "Major, you couldn't discourage me even if you told me it was a grandfather mule."

"On the contrary, Padre," said he, "I would advocate this mule steak to His Majesty himself." (By a strange coincidence, I was to meet the same officer on my way to India several years later. He was then on his way to Afghanistan to train commandos for that country.)

When we returned to our regiment, it was to find ourselves the centre of attention. The platform of ten-inch logs we'd constructed on first arriving at Ortona, and on which we had parked for a month, was blown to hell. Six hours after we left to visit at the hospitals, the enemy had dropped two large shells on our platform, tossing some of the logs ten feet away. We put the logs back in place and parked on the platform until we moved, a month later. As far as I know, we were the only people sleeping above ground, though at least one other shell landed thirty yards away. Because it sank deep in the soft earth, the explosion only created another mudhole which we marked with a stick.

Johnny had a running argument with a friend. They would debate which was right – the army manual covering drivers, or what might be called 'Johnny's common sense'.

Ernie Buss was a modern version of Kipling's Gunga Din. He drove a water truck supplying us with that important commodity. He was very diligent in his duty, and when water was in short supply, as it was in Sicily, he would keep us supplied while other units had long delays. It was in Sicily that we really understood why Kipling's hero really was a hero.

Once in southern Italy, Ernie found a huge supply of cognac. The story goes that he filled his water truck with Italy's best, and made it back to our lines to become a legend in the Third Field Regiment. (Like so many stories that grew in the telling, Ernie later maintained that it was only "a few demijohns" he filled – not a water truck.)

Leaving aside this one exception, it was generally conceded that Ernie stuck fairly close to his army manual. For this reason, he was in constant disagreement with my driver. One day, we overtook Ernie's truck parked near a crossroads, and we presumed the area was being shelled. We spotted Ernie and his helper in slit trenches on the roadside. (That was exactly where the manual said they should be.) Johnny Westine waited until two shells hit the crossroads and then gunned his vehicle through the dangerous spot, stopping several hundred yards beyond. There, hidden from the enemy artillery observer, we got out of our vehicle to watch. We were just in time to observe a direct hit on Ernie's water tanker.

When dusk gathered, the two watermen joined us and we sat down together for one of Johnny's excellent suppers. Westine commented, "Ernie, you will surely get yourself killed if you take that manual too seriously."

To do him justice, Ernie was unimpressed with Johnny's advice. "Westine, I go through more crossroads than you do, and I'm still alive – for me, that's a strong argument."

The fact they both survived the war surely proved something, although I'm not quite sure what.

After supper, we tried to deduce how far we were behind the regiment. Ernie climbed two signposts to see if they would give us a clue. Under the flashlight's glare, he read the disturbing message, "Verges unswept." The second was also enlightening but not too helpful. It read, "Beware snipers." Westine cracked, "That makes interesting reading, Ernie, doesn't it?" We lent them some blankets, and soon we were sleeping like sardines in our little caravan. We caught up with our regiment the next day.

That night Johnny went to a party in one of the dugouts. There he received a rather strange proposition. A gunner said, "Westine, it's obvious the Padre is going to survive this war. But an old sinner like you will never make it. So why don't you sell your job to me in advance? I'll give you fifty thousand lire (sixty dollars) for it. Now I know you can't give me a guarantee, but if you just write a letter to the Padre, to be opened in the event of your death, telling him of our deal, I'll take my chance on that." The deed was done, and he, in turn, sold a second chance to another gunner for ten thousand lire.

16

MUD AND DUGOUTS

The Germans had an advantage. They could decide where they would make a defensive stand. We had to find them and then make our defenses. Even though we had more artillery than the enemy, it usually meant that we didn't have a place to hide from the shells until we had dug in. Besides, I was always a little doubtful about so-called safe hiding places.

One day, after the boys had finished their slit trenches, we had a church service. The enemy left us alone until the middle of my sermon. Then they dropped a big shell a hundred yards away from us. By the time the missile arrived, every one of my congregation had disappeared from sight. I felt very much alone. When it happened a second time, I said, "Listen, you guys, if you keep disappearing I'm going to get six months for talking to myself."

A gunner from Red Deer, Alberta, pulled himself up to a sitting position on the side of his trench and, with a trace of a grin, said, "Padre, do you mind if I answer that question in the morning?"

I managed to find a suitable ending, gave the blessing and flopped down to a prone position as three big 210-mm shells came whining in, landing close to the guns.

When a call for help came, the whole troop leaped out of their foxholes and ran toward the guns. We found that two gunners had been buried by one of the big shells. Their slit trenches were behind a little bank, and the shell, landing in front of the bank, had gone deep, pushing earth over their hiding place. While some went for shovels, others started to dig with their hands. The trenches were five feet deep, but by the time we reached them, both soldiers had suffocated. Everyone had believed those gunners occupied the two safest slit trenches in Italy. From then on, I never trusted slit trenches in general, and deep ones in particular.

This distrust was furthered at Ortona. While the ground was still firm we had dug two slit trenches, or rather, a twin-slit beside our caravan. We were shelled that night. Awakened from a sound sleep, we heard airbursts going off and shell splinters hitting the sides of our caravan. Johnny asked me what I intended to do. I answered that it was dangerous outside as they were using bursts – and so, if I was going to die that night, I was going to at least die in comfort.

In the morning, we found a chunk of steel buried four inches deep in the right-hand side of our trench. We never discussed whose side of the trench got hit, but we did decide that if our time came, it would come in a comfortable bed. We never did use the hole we had dug. And before we left Ortona, it had six inches of water in the bottom.

At Ortona, there was a ridge of sand about twelve feet high and approximately two hundred yards long, covered by a layer of clay. I have no idea of its origin, but our gunners had discovered it, and the south side was honeycombed with dugouts. The sand was firm and the clay covering it shed the rain like an umbrella. The gunners had dug some beautiful living quarters.

There was a bizarre accident when a gunner made a model of our caravan stove, and accidentally set fire to a pile of kindling wood beside it. The owner grabbed a water bottle to douse the flames and discovered, too late, the water bottle was full of Italian cognac. This caused a merry blaze which burned his bedding and most of his belongings. Westine typically commented, "That'll teach them not to take for granted that a water bottle always contains water."

17

THE JUDGEMENT
OF THE GUNNERS

One should never underestimate the power of the private soldier. Lord Wellington understood this. Shortly before the battle was to begin on a field which would give its name to history, the great man was asked about the prospects for the coming battle. Indicating a private soldier who was preparing his musket for action, the Duke made this comment: "The outcome of this battle rests on that article yonder."

When the padres of the First and Second Field were absent because of illness or promotions, I found myself filling in for them as casualties mounted.

The Second Field was a proud unit, and with justification. It had built a reputation from its beginning, in 1939, by dominating competitive anti-tank shooting. Then early in the campaign in Italy, their Commanding Officer, Lt. Col. H.M. Hague, had his right hand cut off by a shell fragment, and he was replaced by Col. L. M. Steuart-Jones. This happened at the height of the heavy fighting early in December at San Leonardo.

Everyone knew the popular old C.O. would be a

hard act to follow. And to complicate matters, the new C.O. made some very bad mistakes in judgement.

As that cold and extremely wet winter progressed, and guns could no longer be dug-in below grade (simply because the pits would fill up with water and collapse), forty thousand sandbags were issued to each regiment including the Second Field. They were to be used to erect low, circular walls around the guns. However, the new C.O. commandeered ten thousand of them to build a shell-proof shelter – providing for his living quarters in one end, and regimental headquarters in the other. He further ensured his safety by roofing it with steel rails covered with more sandbags.

His next act was even more repellent to the battle-seasoned troops. While on an inspection of a battery that had been driven out of drowned slit trenches and were using an old farmhouse (the only whole house in the gun area) as sleeping quarters, he ordered them out into the open. He claimed it would be sheer favouritism if they were allowed to continue to use it. As soon as it was vacant, he set up an officers' mess.

The morale of the regiment plummeted. While there wasn't any ranting, quiet anger, nevertheless, burned with intensity. This often took the form of stories of World War I tyrants being found with a bullet in the back of their head. While I believed these threats were mostly just talk, a way of letting off steam, I counselled moderation, and hoped and prayed they'd take my advice.

After three months of bitter fighting, the division was taken out of the line. Our Brigadier ordered a competitive practice tank shoot among the three field regiments. The results were startling. The Second Field was not only the worst of the three, but it failed to make one hit during the entire day.

I later overheard the comments the C.O. made to the Brigadier, as they stood on the other side of a thick hedge. He was telling the Brigadier what he was going to do to whip them into shape.

But the Brigadier stopped him in mid-sentence: "Colonel, if a regiment becomes as bad as yours, the Colonel is always at least part of the cause. Your gunners were sending a message direct to me, and I am removing you from your command as of now. I will appoint your successor immediately, and you will collect your kit and come back with me to headquarters now."

Such was the power of Canadian gunners when they reached a consensus on their leadership. How many officers were given adverse reports because of the actions of their troops on manoeuvres in England, no one will ever know. But they were many in number, I am certain.

There was also a generous side to Canadian gunners. They were always ready to extend help to anyone they thought deserving.

When I returned to the Third Field, I found a number of men from the Seventy-seventh Battery, from Moose Jaw, helping an Italian farmer with a threshing operation. This old fellow had the most ancient steam engine I had ever seen, and a threshing separator which was at least as old. Three of the boys from the Third Field had taken over the running of the engine. They were assisted in this by Ernie Buss's water truck and a jeep hauling wood to fire the boiler. No less than five men were operating the separator. They had to manufacture several pulleys and other parts which had worn out, so they brought up the expert mechanics and machinists of the L.A.D. Four or five top mechanics worked hard, making parts, belts and pulleys, for the machine that had far outlived the time when such parts could be purchased.

It had been threatening rain all day long. At five o'clock in the afternoon, the last sheaf had gone through the mill when an old steam whistle suddenly sounded. It hadn't worked for years, but under the care of a mechanic from the L.A.D., it suddenly piped a triumphant cry, telling everyone the two-day job was finished. Then the rain came down in torrents. The old farmer was ecstatic and called on all the Saints to bless the Canadian Army. Indeed, he went one better – he produced a massive feast for the twenty-three men who had taken part in the threshing bee. I was invited to join the feast, although I hadn't done anything but blow the whistle.

We were seated at two long tables in the large living room, while servants heaped our plates with spaghetti and meat sauce. Then we were served a giant salad with an olive oil dressing. I nearly accepted a second helping, until someone warned me that the main course was still to come. When the last of the pasta had disappeared, four men came in carrying a huge table with twelve roast geese on it. These were served with potatoes and several Italian vegetable dishes. This, in turn, was followed by a delicious Italian dessert and great pots of Espresso coffee, which I believe was a gift from the gunners. Two huge demijohns of Vino Rosso flowed freely throughout the meal.

It was by far the best meal I had in Italy. Actually, it was more than just a good meal – it was a kind of miracle. The old mill had threshed the biggest harvest the old farmer had enjoyed in years. He got up to make a speech, but he broke down and cried. He kept repeating, "It is a miracle. It is a miracle –you Canadians are a miracle. How you kept that old machine going, I'll never know."

Well, I know. He had put himself in the hands of the Third Canadian Field Regiment – it was as simple as that!

For the men of the Seventy-seventh Battery it was a grand day. Everyone felt great about what had happened, and it gave us a much-needed lift of morale. For two days it took us away from the mud, noise and heartache of war, back to something which reminded us of home.

18

CASA BIANCA

Now and then, Regimental Headquarters managed to hole up in a reputable building. But the finest, from my point of view, was Casa Bianca, on the road to Rimini. It was here, too, that I really became acquainted with a gunner with a gargantuan appetite.

The driver of an ammunition lorry returned one day to the regiment with forty-eight Italian eggs, which, though smaller than small Canadian eggs, still constituted a treasure trove. He was just a tad late for lunch, and we saw him counting the crowd. Finally, he said, "Fellows, I'm sad to say I am two eggs short to let each of you have one, and it would break my heart to leave even one of you out in the cold. So I've decided to eat all the eggs myself and preserve our friendship. I've appointed my friend Pete to cook the eggs, and all the rest of you can watch along with Zeke."

Now Zeke was a sad-faced hound dog who had the reputation of being the only member of the Third Field with a bigger appetite that his master. Zeke lay close by and watched as Pete fried great panfuls of eggs in olive oil for his big friend, who speared them one at a time with his fork and popped them in his mouth. When he had eaten about two dozen eggs, Zeke's big, sad eyes got the best of his master, and he said, "All right, son, open up." In quick succession, he tossed the next six to his dog, who, not even bothering to get up, opened his cavernous mouth and received this largess with quiet dignity. The gunner ate the remaining eggs after supper that same day. All of us watched in awe as he finished the very last one. Then he drawled, "I'd miss dessert any time for this."

The owner of Casa Bianca, a family of high estate, was a close relative of the Italian royal family. We were warned by the higher authorities that untoward behaviour would be heavily frowned upon and treated with swift justice. The owners did not vacate the building when we were billeted there, but retired to one wing of this four-storeyed home. The quarters assigned to me were on the fourth floor, and seeing them, I expressed surprise at their size. All in all, they took up a fifteen- by twenty-foot space. When I asked the Adjutant why I didn't have to share them with another officer, he grinned and said, "Padre, everybody would like to be there, but the owner specified it was to be yours and yours alone. You see, the remainder of the attic is occupied by his attractive daughter, and the owner doesn't want to have someone trying to break the wall down."

The partition was made of eight- by four-foot sheeting, but it was only one board thick. While it was quite secure, you could easily follow a conversation on the other side. This factor proved to be a mixed blessing.

The daughter, who had the title of Marquessa, was served by a young woman occupying a room or alcove at the entrance to the Marquessa's stairway. The state of the acoustics was somewhat embarrassing. Occupants beyond the partition were totally unaware they could be overheard, never hearing any conversation from my side. I tended to be absent most of the time, and when I was there I was alone and so, naturally, never spoke.

Late one night, I was surprised to hear a man's voice on the other side of the wallboard. Then, I heard the lady saying, "You know, if my father finds you here he will kill you."

"Ma'am, every day I risk my life for a much less important reason."

The man's voice had the sound of prairie stubble about it, and I made an educated guess as to the owner's identity. The soldier left the apartment at three o'clock.

The next day I examined the outside of our building. A narrow beam ran from the roof of a barn-like building to a narrow ledge on the top floor of the house. It appeared to be six inches square, and fifteen or twenty long. The beam had wires on top of it, and it followed that anyone using it for travel would have to go hand over hand along its edge, braving the possibility of a twenty-five foot drop to the ground below. Nevertheless, the intruder made at least four further visits during our stay in the Casa. I never could make up my mind which would be worse – that the intruder should be discovered by an outraged father, or that he should fall twenty-five feet from an ancient beam.

While nothing happened to the nocturnal visitor next door, the Casa was the scene of one tragic accident. A visiting mine expert became interested in a new type of mine shown him by his driver. Whether or not he tried to open it, we shall never know, but they were both blown into small fragments when it detonated. I missed being with them by a minute or so.

On my way to my vehicle, I had been stopped by a regimental cook, who was having problems with his wife in Ontario. That day I was in a hurry to get somewhere. I listened to him for three or four minutes and then, excusing myself rather abruptly, started out of the Casa. As I reached the door, there was a tremendous explosion outside. I was knocked down and my ears were ringing. When I got on my feet, I went out to find that the Major's jeep had been transformed into a pile of junk, and the officer and his driver had been blown apart. A large piece of heavy back muscle was lying close to the door of the Casa, twitching as if it were alive. Our caravan had been called into the L.A.D. for repairs, and the replacement vehicle was parked eight feet or so from the Major's jeep. The left side of the machine had been pushed in as if it had been hit by a giant fist.

While I waited for our Adjutant, I went back into the Casa, called the gunner cook, and said, "Please, tell me all about your wife."

Had he not detained me, I might have been looking over the Major's shoulder when the mine went off.

This was the kind of crazy world we lived in, in the mountains of Italy. Witnessing this tragedy made one great change in my life. I never again was too busy to listen to a story, however dull. I noted a similar mellowing in the attitude of Johnny Westine. Up until then, he had often intimated that I was a bit of a pushover, giving extra listening time to gunners. I noted that, later, he gave the cook a prized tin of old cheddar cheese he'd received from home.

19

THE FAITH OF GEORGE SPENCER

His name wasn't really Rene Leblanc, but I shall refer to him as such. He hailed from a small town on the north shore of the St. Lawrence in Quebec. The youngest son in a family of twelve, he was born with a speech difficulty due to a restriction of his tongue. People said he was "tongue-tied," a condition which could have been rectified by any ordinary general practitioner, but was overlooked in a big family trying to survive the Great Depression.

Everyone knew he spoke queerly, but no one had detected the reason. The family could understand what he said, but his disability was treated as a kind of joke, except by Rene. To him it was not funny. It was humiliation – it was pain – it was deep and abiding anger.

Then, at the age of six, he went to school. Each of the new pupils had to stand up and say their name. When it was his turn, Rene stood up and said, "My name if Rene Leblanc." This was followed by a shocked silence, after which the teacher stood up, and crossing her eyes, repeated what he had said, mimicking his garbled tone. Everyone rocked with laughter.

The small boy fled from the school and never returned. His mother taught him to add, subtract and multiply. This was the sum of his education. He did chores for the local doctor's wife, earning a few cents a day. He was ragged by his older brothers, who tried to make him lose his temper and then mimicked his outbursts. In addition, he had started to stutter the day he ran away from school.

Eventually, at the age of sixteen, he got a job in the paper mill. It was not much of a job, but it gave him a vestige of self-respect. The ragging of his brothers went on though, and he was more and more turned-in on himself. He told me that the happy moments of his life were so few that he could remember all of them.

At the time of his eighteenth birthday, he went to Quebec City and enlisted in the army. He had hoped to go overseas with a reinforcement group and get himself posted to the famous Vingt-Deux Regiment, as he had very little English. Instead, he was sent to the Third Canadian Field Regiment. Later, he told me that he had considered this to be just one more in his history of disasters. Here he was, in a western artillery regiment where English was the only language spoken, and where even the few francophones there could hardly understand his garbled French. In the midst of this chaos and catastrophe, he met George Spencer, the Official Educational Sergeant of the regiment. With this meeting, his life was turned around completely, and a miracle began to take shape.

To begin with, George Spencer was the first person Rene had ever met who was interested in him as a person. George also had a family member or acquaintance who had been tongue-tied and had overcome the disability. He told Rene that he would help him overcome his difficulties, including his stuttering, and he would teach him mathematics, as well as to speak English.

He took Rene to Harley Street in London, to one of the best throat specialists in that street of famous doctors. The doctor freed Rene's tongue. He warned George that Rene would have to learn to speak all over again, and to deal with the stuttering as well. "It's a long, hard road, Mr. Spencer, but if anyone can do it, I think it will be you."

It was at this time that I came to the regiment and was immediately drafted as Educational Officer. Thus, technically, I became George Spencer's supervisor.

Our first problem was – how do you cure a man of stuttering? I didn't even realize that this was strictly the work of a speech pathologist. A measure of my ignorance of the subject was first that I thought we could help him, and second that I had to go back to Greek history to get even one idea, which was surely scraping the bottom of the barrel. I told them about the story of the man named Demosthenes, who cured his stuttering by speaking with pebbles in his mouth, and went on to become an orator of note.

Rene put pebbles in his mouth and didn't stutter, but neither could he speak understandably. By doing this, though, I discovered that if he spoke while he was smiling, he could restrain the stuttering somewhat. This inadvertently got him in trouble with our R.S.M., however. The R.S.M., finding some fault with his appearance on parade, questioned Rene. In order to answer, Rene grinned from ear to ear, moving the R.S.M. to wrath, "Get that silly grin off your face, or I'll wipe it off."

As soon as Rene obeyed the order he was totally speechless.

I spoke to the R.S.M. and he consented not to ask Rene

questions on parade for three months. In turn, I promised to give the great man a monthly report on the matter. Within that time Rene learned to smile 'inside' and obtain the same result.

In the meantime, George gave him hours and hours of teaching, and at the end of the war he had brought the young man from Grade Two arithmetic to a real mastery of arithmetic, algebra and differential calculus. George affirmed that Rene was one of the three best mathematics students he had ever known.

At the end of the war in Europe, I, being single, was assigned to the Expeditionary Force to go to the Far East. When I said good-bye to Rene Leblanc, he was the personification of a beautiful miracle. I told him I was very happy with what he and George had accomplished. He replied, "The most important thing that ever happened to me was that I was sent to this regiment and met George and you."

He spoke in a calm, low voice, with not a trace of a stutter. He spoke English with hardly a trace of an accent and was completely in control. I said that his family would be surprised when he got home.

"Yes," he said, "they will indeed, and now I can easily get a job as an accountant at the mill because I will be bilingual. *And, I will write my brothers' pay cheques!* Above all, I am happy and proud of myself and I have left anger behind me forever." It was the most beautiful miracle I have ever witnessed.

George Spencer was a Mormon from southern Alberta. He came overseas with the Ninety-second Battery of the Third Field Regiment. Most people conceded he was a poor soldier, but a first-class teacher. He was prepared to work day and night for the welfare of his students. He certainly was the best Educational Sergeant in our division, or perhaps the whole army.

When we landed in Italy, he soon felt the heavy hand of the new R.S.M., who lived by the book. When someone told him about George, his abilities and weak points, this 'spit and polish' soldier made a pronouncement: "If someone could teach him to be a good teacher, I will teach him to be a good soldier." George started to present himself on parade every morning after breakfast – even in rest areas. Each of these was a humiliating disaster for George.

One night, his buddies determined this was going to stop. They took George over. They gave his boots a high shine, they polished his brass, they worked on his webbing, and they pressed his tunic and pants. They also did a special job on his rifle. When he came on parade, he was immaculate!

The parade was called on a cobblestone square in an Italian village. One cobblestone was missing, and in its place was a little pool of silt and water. George was standing in line right beside the hole, and when he ordered arms, the butt of his rifle came down in the tiny sea of mud. When he sloped arms, a large glob of mud came up with the rifle butt and squeezed out between George's fingers.

Somehow the R.S.M. had learned of the help George had received, and when he saw the glob of mud, he said, "Sergeant what do you mean coming on parade with a dirty rifle?" His glee showed in his voice, and set in motion a cold and calculated determination to get rid of this 'spit and polish' Warrant Officer. The fact that he was nearing the age limit for field work was going to make this easier. More of this later.

And George Spencer was the man who worked the miracle with Rene Leblanc – within one big frame, this man was the best teacher and the worst soldier in the Canadian Army. Some of his comrades would have added that he was also the most naïve member of ours or, indeed, any army in the world. As one of the boys put it, "There's no fun in playing a trick on George – he will find some way to praise you for it and make you think you should join the Salvation Army." As a result, many a practical joker dismantled his prize trick before his victim could fall into the trap set for him.

George's trip to Harley Street was typical of the magic of the man. No one else would have dared to go there to ask for a favour, and few, if any, would have been able to stir up faith in, or receive the advice he did from, that holiest of holy of the medical world. The great medic understood the magic of total trust and caring unmarred by the slightest guile. He knew that what Rene needed, above all, was a friend who cared deeply and had faith that could move mountains. And to his amazement he saw all these things in this unbelievably naïve Canadian – George Spencer.

One day, George asked for permission to travel to the town of Reggio, where he had heard there was a great supply of books. I believe they were meant for the American Army. George, though, believed teaching exceeded nationality, and he not only went to Reggio, but convinced the Americans to give him several hundred books to aid him in his great mission. Had he been able to get them into his great pack, he would have carried them back. As it was, he entrusted his precious books to the Army Service Corps, and they were delivered to the regiment twelve days before George made it back himself.

His return was delayed because he was arrested by the British Provost as he passed through Rome. It would no doubt be helpful at this time to explain that George was about six feet tall and weighed over two hundred pounds. You could describe him as heavyset, with blondish hair and startling blue eyes. He had sloping shoulders and, as someone put it, he made a uniform look bad. The Americans thought he was a German spy, and they called in the British Provost. Taken to headquarters, he was questioned. "Sergeant, what is the name of your Commanding Officer?"

"I'm afraid I don't know. You see, I always just call him 'Sir'."

"Who is your Adjutant?'

"I don't know his name either, but he is a medium-sized officer with blonde hair and his first name is Earl. I don't know what his last name is."

"Sergeant, why are you not wearing a forage cap?"

"Sir, I gave mine to a chap who was about to be arrested by the Provost. He told me he would bring it back, but I suppose he couldn't make it."

Understandably, the British Provost doubted his story, and he was lodged in a single cell in one of the local jails. Meanwhile, they worked on the premise that he was a German spy. Perhaps this was understandable; he did look very German.

At this time, the Italian authorities also saw fit to arrest several hundred prostitutes from the streets of Rome and lodge them in the same prison in which George was held. These ladies occupied a huge cell right beside him. Puzzled by their presence, he could only say, "They couldn't all have been spies."

The ladies had their own questions about George Spencer. They gathered around his cell, regaling him with all sorts of requests and outbursts of Romanese Italian.

This drew loud cheers and hilarious outbursts of laughter from others of their group.

About this time, George asked for an interview with the Commanding Officer of the Provost, and offered this suggestion to him: "Sir, I am a teacher by profession, and if it's necessary for me to remain in your custody, I would like to make myself helpful and earn my keep. Would you give me permission to teach the members of the guard who are off duty?"

Intrigued, the C.O. took him to the guards' quarters and let him make his offer. Spencer made his pitch:

"Gentlemen, I am a math teacher by profession, and algebra is a very exciting subject. Would all who care to explore this subject with me, please write your name on this pad, and we will have our first class this evening."

To the C.O.'s amazement, every soldier in the guard signed up for the class, and at the week's end their enthusiasm had not flagged. He therefore called our regiment and asked for the adjutant. The following is the gist of the conversation:

Provost Officer: "Sir, could I speak to the Adjutant of theThird Canadian Field Regiment?"

The Adjutant: "Captain Clemis, Adjutant of the Third Field speaking."

Provost Officer: "Captain, do you have an Education . . . "

Clemis: "By the name of Sergeant George Spencer. And he doesn't know my name, right?"

Provost Officer: "Right."

Clemis: "He's ours – our one and only – and if I am right, he is teaching some of your people mathematics, right?"

Provost Officer: "Right, and Captain Clemis, to use a

delightful Canadian expression, he's driving us all nuts. We'll send him up to you tomorrow, special delivery."

20

AND THEN THERE WAS A GUY NAMED JOHNSON

Johnson was a war casualty. He was never wounded – in fact, he seemed to live a charmed life. He was also quite fearless. I often wondered what a psychiatric assessment would have produced. Long before he fell foul of the law, I had come to the conclusion that he was completely amoral. At the same time he was friendly in a limited sort of way.

The north of Italy is a land of canals and rivers, and one of the most impossible places I know for waging war. The winter brought on a sort of stalemate when the enemy blew all the bridges. We settled down to living in the discomfort of a land which has its harvest rains in the winter.

Several nights a week, Johnson would go out in the evening and disappear for four or five hours. He would appear the next day with an assortment of enemy equipment, pistols, cameras, knives and other such things.

As time went on, we learned that he would swim across a canal or river, hide near an enemy outpost, and wait for an enemy to walk along the trail. Then he would hit his victim on the head with a piece of steel pipe and rob the body of money or whatever he might find. Often, he would leave an Italian grenade around to mislead the enemy. He gave me a pair of Zeiss binoculars, saying lightly, "Padre, how would you like these field glasses? I picked them up for a song." I insisted on giving him ten dollars, which was only a fraction of their value. He didn't want to accept any payment. Eventually, when I became aware of their origin, I gave them away.

His night journeys continued all winter, and at least once he ambushed an enemy patrol, killing five soldiers with an enemy automatic weapon. He came back laden with loot. Then he had a couple of close calls when the enemy tried to ambush him. After that he cut short his sorties and lived a fairly normal life. All went well. He did his duties, taking his turn on guard duty, and was noted as an excellent chap to get things done in a hurry.

Soon, however, he started to drink rather heavily, and people noted that he was more withdrawn than before. It was at this time that a murder took place in an Italian house near the regiment. The mother said two soldiers came to the door, one of them carrying a tommy gun. When her husband went to the door, a soldier demanded Vino Rosso. She said her husband said "no," and shut the door and locked it. The soldier fired his automatic through the door, killing her husband. They then kicked the door in. One went to the wine cellar and carried away a five-gallon bottle of wine – the other grabbed one of her daughters and raped her.

The Commanding Officer paraded a number of soldiers in front of the women and they picked out two immediately. Johnson was recognized as the man who shot her husband. Both were arrested and sent to the army prison. The Provost were called and came for the prisoners. The Sergeant-Major spoke to the young Provost Officer and told him that Johnson was no ordinary prisoner and would escape if they were not careful. He added, "He is clever, resourceful and mean."

To this the young officer replied, "Sergeant-Major, prisoners don't escape from us."

As soon as I heard of the arrests, I went to visit the prisoners, and said, "Johnson, you sure blew the lid off this time."

"Yes, Padre," he answered, "I have two charges against me. I'm up for murder, but the second is really hard to beat. I'm charged with being A.W.O.L."

The way he said it, I knew he wasn't sorry he'd committed murder, only angry that he had been caught. It was impossible to break through this façade of nonchalance.

The first staging area was about thirty miles behind the lines. It consisted of two barbed wire fences about nine feet high. The inner one was electrified, and within it was one big building that could, if necessary, hold about thirty prisoners. Beside this was a small building with bars, presumably for-high risk prisoners.

Johnson was put in the small building by himself at about three o'clock. He immediately stood beside the door which faced the gate. Here he observed the movements and drills of the guard, and the times of changes. He presumed the guard would change at six o'clock after a six-hour shift, and he noted that one guard was posted outside the building.

Having learned the routine of the guard, Johnson waited until a quarter to six, then lay down on the floor and started to moan. The guard, thinking he had taken poison, came into the room and, kneeling over him, asked what he had taken. This was what the prisoner was waiting for. He slugged the soldier, knocking him out with one blow. He then changed into the guard's uniform, tied and gagged the man, took his rifle and started marching back and forth in front of the cell. When six o'clock and darkness came, he marched out of the gate after the new guard came on duty. When the old guard were dismissed, he just kept on walking. He had been in prison exactly three hours.

Johnson hitched a ride back up to the front, passed through the Canadian lines, picked up some kit from his bunker, and established himself in a house out in the 'no man's land' between the two armies. It was a large house which had been badly damaged, but the kitchen area was intact. There was debris on the roof, but it was quite waterproof. He found a small Italian pistol which he used to shoot chickens, young pigs and game which had been cultured by a landowner. He also managed to get his hands on some Canadian army supplies, and was able to live quite well for several months.

The broken part of the house provided an abundance of firewood. In addition, he found a cache of German beer, which he consumed with some discretion. To protect himself, he picked up some German mine signs and placed them strategically around his house. On one occasion, he watched nervously as a German night patrol came right up to the building. He was getting ready to use his automatic, but the mine warning did the trick – the patrol withdrew.

Then one day, he splurged. He ate a whole chicken, drank the rest of his beer and went to sleep. He was rudely awakened, to use his own words, "looking up the wrong end of a Schmeisser." He told someone after the war that the patrol leader had congratulated him on his set-up. At the end of the war, he was handed over to the Canadian Provost. The death sentence he had received "in absentia" was commuted to life imprisonment.

21

AN AWESOME SILENCE

The war was, for me, a devastating experience. I am convinced that, had it lasted, I might well have become a psychological and spiritual casualty. Probably the only reason I survived the brutish and senseless things that happened was because they were interspersed with the humour and good will of the ordinary soldier.

One day, as the division was being assembled to move forward, I had to leave my driver and go to the rear of our regiment. To get back to my driver, I hitched a ride with one of the gun crews in their quad, which was pulling an ammunition limber and a gun. Altogether, the hitch-up was forty-one-feet long. As we approached my caravan, I asked the driver to slow down to ten m.p.h. and said, "I'll be seeing you, fellows."

I stepped off the side of the quad and ran a few steps to my vehicle. Westine had the door already open, and I stepped into the vehicle just as it moved forward. We broke into the convoy two vehicles behind the quad I had just left. We had just established our position when a shell hit that quad, landing on the six tins of petrol fastened to the roof.

The explosion pierced hundreds of holes in the tins and the roof of the cab, wounding all the crew, spraying them with gasoline and setting them on fire. The driver pulled his vehicle off the road and down over a twenty-foot bank to the riverbed below. Such was the skill of the driver, that he took the whole long train down the perpendicular bank without upsetting anything. There they all piled out and tried in vain to put their blazing clothing out by rolling in the sand. They all died, including the heroic driver.

When I came back to the site early the next day, I could see where one of them had crawled sixty feet to a sandbank hoping to find water. When he got there and realized there wasn't any water, he had punched the sand with his fist in frustration, then laid his head down and died. Even though water might not have helped all that much, I could imagine his frustration and his pain.

There were signs everywhere on that Italian riverbed of the last part of their drama of life and death. Although I had known them intimately for several years, I still marvelled at how very young they looked – younger, indeed, than they had when I had said good-bye to them minutes before their fiery deaths.

The gunner who had crawled out to the sandbank had thrown his helmet away before he had punched the sand. I brought it back to him, brushed the sand out of his curly brown hair and put the helmet back on his head. Then I waited for the party which came to pick up the bodies. Deep inside I felt sick and discouraged, and very, very lonely. I wept in the honesty of solitude.

Then there was the tragedy of the First Field Regiment, the Royal Canadian Horse Artillery. Word came that a gunner had gone berserk, and shot and killed four sergeants. One of these was the son of George and Mabel Hunter of Petawawa. I knew them well and wrote to send them my love. It seemed much worse for their son to die that way than to be killed by the enemy. Mabel Hunter was a beautiful person, and she bore this crushing blow with courage and dignity.

One evening, a young gunner came and told me his fears. He said, "Padre, if anything happens to me it will kill my mother; Father went to France in the First World War, before I was born. I never saw him, and he never saw me. What a rotten break it would be if she lost me too. In spite of that, I don't want to leave the regiment, but I hope for her sake I make it back."

The next day, one shell landed in our lines. The young gunner was in a tent typing a letter. One piece of the shell splinter pierced the wall of the tent and hit him in the spine. He was dead before we got to him.

I wrote ten letters to his mother and tore each one up. Finally I wrote one, signed and sealed it, and sent it off. Some weeks later I got a reply, one of the bravest letters I ever received. She said that she had been richly blessed by having gained the love of two of the finest men that ever lived. She said, "You knew my son well. His father was just like him. I know many women who have lived a whole lifetime and never known what I have known, and have never been blessed as I have been blessed."

This lady added to my conviction that women have a great and wondrous inner strength and courage.

Once, in Italy, I saw a Spitfire come down in an olive orchard. The plane's wings were too wide to land between the rows of olive trees, and the tips were broken off. When the landing gear contacted the ground, it sank in the soft earth, causing the plane to brake sharply. This pulled the engine of the plane off its mountings, and it came to rest forty feet ahead. I was scarcely one hundred feet away from the plane when the fuselage came to a full stop. I ran, with difficulty, through the ploughed field toward it. When I reached the plane, I saw that a small fire was burning under the wing, and the pilot was turning his head from side to side as smoke gathered in the cockpit.

I tried to open the cockpit, but I didn't have anything with which to lever the canopy open or smash the Plexiglass. I could only punch it with my fists in frustration. As I was doing this, an explosive of some sort went off under the seat and threw the pilot straight up, taking the canopy off with him. His body fell back to earth headfirst, and he didn't move again. I had experienced a deep and abiding frustration as I tried unsuccessfully to set this incredibly young British pilot free. Part of me died with him on that muddy Italian field.

One of the most difficult experiences of my life was when every member of a gun crew died in one tragic accident. There is a set drill for loading and firing a twenty-five-pounder gun. One gunner lays the shell in the breech of the gun, and another pushes it into the gun, ramming it with a wooden rammer until it engages in the rifling of the barrel. A third gunner puts the cartridge containing the propellant into the breech as it closes. Finally, the gunner who lays the gun on line pulls the firing lever.

One crew didn't follow this drill. The gunner who put the shell into the breech threw it with such force that it engaged in the rifling without a rammer. This sped things up but was not a safe procedure. On this particular day, the loader hit the breech of the gun with the shell, and it exploded. The built-in safety factors in the fuse didn't work with that particular shell.

Two of the crew were blown to pieces and all the others killed. We spent the rest of the day gathering up the broken fragments of the two bodies. There were literally hundreds of pieces of flesh thrown in all directions by the explosion. Some stuck on trees twenty feet up from the ground. We also knew that for as much as we found, probably as much more was not found. It was one of the truly horrible days of my life.

From the day that happened forty-five years ago, each time I celebrate the Holy Eucharist and say the words, "This is my body, which is broken for you," my thoughts go back to that awful day of breaking and gathering, and I feel the old pain all over again.

One of the things which helped the army to survive in the face of death, destruction, cold, mud and loneliness was the discovery of caring among the members of the regiment.

One day at a place called San Pietro, one of our gun crews, led by a Sergeant called Fat Moore, was wiped out. At the time of their death I was engaged elsewhere. When Johnny and I arrived on the scene, the crew had been buried, and someone had erected five crosses. We collected some cup-sized stones, and Johnny Westine produced from his store of wonders some whitewash, with which he coated the stones and crosses. He also trimmed the crosses with a saw to make them more uniform. We knew that the bodies would have to be moved, but the whole regiment appreciated that the graves looked neat and clean. Friends of the dead came and took pictures to send back to Canada. Finally, someone (I believe it was a photographer for *Saturday Night*) sent a picture back to Canada. The whole regiment was pleased and proud when friends sent copies of the paper back to Italy. It was a real family pride.

On Christmas day, we were dug in on the Fortunato Ridge. We were hoping for an action-free Christmas. The boys had arranged a festive dinner, and I had arranged a Christmas Eucharist for ten o'clock. The sun rose in hazy splendour, and we anticipated a peaceful day to celebrate the birth of Our Lord. The boys had found a grassy place for the altar, which was made of boxes of live ammunition covered with a tarp. A flag served as an altar frontal. On top of this was a linen altar covering and a full array of spotlessly white altar linen. The boys gathered round, intrigued to look closely at the only white cloth they had seen in months and months. In the meantime, several gunners pushed a line of ammunition cases firmly down in the mud and rolled some empty sand bags as cushions. They placed them on top of the ammo boxes, making a comfortable place to kneel to receive the blessed sacrament.

We started the service with 150 men present. About five minutes into the service, a single gun sounded. To this day, I don't know if it was our side or the enemy who was the guilty party, but all hell broke loose. Half of my congregation were called away to the guns. I couldn't even hear the sound of my own voice. The concussion of our own guns snuffed out the altar candles, and the ground shook so much I had to steady the chalice.

Then suddenly, in the middle of the Gospel reading,

125

there was an awesome silence as I read these words: "He was in the world and the world was made by him and the world knew him not; he came unto his own and his own received him not, but to as many as received him, to them he gave power to become the sons of God even to as many as believed on his name."

Then the noise came crashing back, blotting out the remainder of the Eucharist.

The great silence was only sixteen seconds long, but it was very impressive, and a hundred Canadians would remember it for a very long time. Forty years later, at a reunion in Surrey, British Columbia, there were veterans who still remembered the "great silence."

22

THE WEATHER AND MOODS OF ITALY

No people are more attuned to the weather than the people of Italy, swinging from joy to a sombre mood and back again, with the changing seasons. Perhaps I should qualify that by saying we observed this among the people of the mountainous parts of the country where we spent two winters, and where most of the precipitation falls as rain – cold, miserable rain, producing endless acres of mud.

It is the only time of the year when the ordinary citizens do not sing. They crowd into their dwellings and gather around tiny fires. Even though it was a time when burdens were piled onto civilians, the war never kept people from singing at any other time of the year. In the wintertime, every man, woman and child seemed obsessed with the single determination to survive. In every little town and village, the local restaurant produced torrents of scalding hot and very potent coffee. They seemed to consider it a survival necessity, only second in importance to Vino Rosso.

In Italy, winter is always associated with mud. Cities, towns and villages, and even some tiny hamlets, dealt with this problem by setting down cobblestones as pavement. Indeed, it may have been the mud that prompted the Romans and their descendants to become such master road-builders. Without good roads, communications would have been severely restricted, if not totally prohibited. Mud, rain and cold drove man and beast indoors for the duration of the winter – no singing, no dancing – only a never-ending struggle to survive a most unkind season.

However, when spring came, it unleashed unbridled joy and singing. The flowers, the trees, the insects and birds, the brilliant sunshine and the sound of laughter flooded the whole of life behind the lines with irrepressible joy. Every time we approached a town or village, we could hear the vibrant notes of spring. The laughter of the children, the bawling of the cattle, the calling of domestic fowl, all these added to the chorus of spring.

Happy springtime sounds tumbled across the colourful countryside with its patchwork of little fruit and vegetable farms. From the highest mountain village to the fields of the lowlands, the voices of children and the music of the country blended in happy union, and as the summer progressed, the vegetables and fruits ripened.

Harvest time filled everyone's life. It was a busy time, and yet no one seemed to mind the heavy burdens of the working day. Grain was cut and carried on carts to fill barns and sheds, ready for threshing time. Sometimes the animals did the threshing by walking round and round over the sheaves until the grain was separated from the stalks and chaff. High in the mountains, the work was done with wooden flails, wielded by workers. In the vineyards, barefoot young women trod the grapes in vats, sinking thigh-deep in the purple mash. Autumn was a time of intensive labour but it was a labour of love, and it was a

128

labour of song and dance. In every restaurant, or even outdoors, people sang and listened. You could not help but hear the sound of music. It mingled with every hour of work. It filled the workers as they worked; indeed, it was of the work itself.

But then came the grey skies of December and the cold, bitter rain day after day. The singing, music and laughter ceased as the Italians moved inside to their state of semi-hibernation.

The troops, however, couldn't move inside and hibernate. It will always amaze me how we were able to adapt to the wretched weather. One day for instance, I came across a gunner standing in the pouring rain, eating alternately from two mess tins – one containing M and V stew, and the other canned rice pudding, a real delicacy. When I asked him why on earth he was eating this way, he explained that, logically, if he waited until he finished the stew, the rice pudding would be overflowing and ruined by rainwater.

So used to the eternal rain did we become that one day, near the end of the winter of 1944, I actually sat down and had tea in the pouring rain with the Padre of the Seaforth Highlanders. We were at a crossroads which was being shelled, and as usual, Johnny Westine had stopped his vehicle and listened to the guns. Deciding there were, as usual, two enemy guns working as a battery, he started his engine and waited until two shells landed. Then he raced through at high speed before the smoke cleared away. We stopped behind some cover and saw two more shells come in, landing where we had been less than half a minute before.

It was then that I saw smoke rising from a row of roofless houses. I walked across and rapped on one of the doors. A voice replied, "Come in." I opened the door to see Padre Roy Durnford of the Seaforth Highlanders, glistening wet, sitting at a table in a spot he had cleared of rubble. He had made tea in a blue Royal Doulton teapot and was drinking out of a delicate cup, also a survivor of the shelling. Looking up, he said, "Padre – come in out of the rain – you'll get soaking wet out there." I accepted his invitation, entered his roofless house and shared his pot of English tea, drinking from another survivor of the Royal Doulton family.

During our conversation, I questioned Roy as to who was stationed in the area. "Davie," he answered, "there are only two kinds of people here – the quick and the dead." I wondered at the resilience of this unique character. He was, I knew, heartbroken at the immense losses recently suffered by his regiment.

The Seaforth Highlanders was a proud regiment with a proud record. In one engagement, they were to spearhead an attack on the enemy line. They had pinpointed all the enemy guns and mortars, and the field artillery supporting them had zeroed in on all the targets and were ready for a heavy barrage once the attack was mounted. Unfortunately, the enemy brought in four four-inch mortars and had registered them, ready for the Seaforth's expected attack.

When the attack developed, our fire power nullified the known enemy guns and mortars, but the new mortars remained hidden until the Seaforths started their attack. Each quickly dropped three rounds into the advancing infantry. Fifty-six men fell dead in a field scarcely seventy-five feet square. It was impossible to walk across it without stepping over several bodies.

I knew that Roy Durnford was deeply hurt by this

tragedy. But finding two cups and a teapot that had survived in these smashed and roofless houses was enough to evoke the kind of humour which was life itself to all of us on active service. Hundreds of dishes had been destroyed by our shelling, but two usable chairs and a table, two cups and a teapot had moved him to search for a silver spoon. Then he cleared the rubble from six feet square of floor and produced a civilized tea party. The miraculous appearance of four Danish cookies from his pocket put the finishing touch to a truly wondrous miracle. As we sat in the gentle rain partaking of this civilized social grace, our spirits were lifted with renewed hope for the future of mankind.

23

A MEASURE OF A MAN

It was during the late winter of 1943, or early spring of 1944, when the morale of our regiment reached its lowest ebb. I had seen this happen previously in the Second Field Regiment when the men were in conflict with their C.O. But this was something different. It involved the whole division and was directly related to the fact that our soldiers on the Italian front were feeling forgotten as the world's attention was transferred to Normandy. The Senior Padre of our division suggested we meet with the men and try to address the problem. The meetings were called "The Padre's Hour," and were very enlightening.

The first meeting began with a strained silence. Nobody wanted to talk. Then one N.C.O. dropped the bomb.

"I've been over here for damned near five years. I have a kid who will be starting school in September. I've never seen him, except in pictures. He asks his mother if I love him, and when she says yes, he says, `then why doesn't he come to see us?'

"'Bill,' she says, 'I'm running out of answers – and I don't believe the ones I'm giving him. I know you are fighting for your country, but surely the time comes when a father should be able to see his kids and wife. Surely it's not right for one soldier to be away for four and a half years, and another in Canada all that time. I know that you have to be away, but Bill, I'm tired – I'm angry – and I'm lonely. I haven't seen you for four and a half years, which is nine times as long as we were together married. I didn't mean to bitch about all this. I'll try not to do it again. Come when you can. We will be waiting.'"

This sad story stirred up a maelstrom of emotions culminating in outrage. Over and over again it was a similar tale – long years of fear and loneliness and despair. Now and then, throughout these "Padre's Hours," anger boiled over, and some hard words were spoken, and hard questions asked. Mostly, though, there was quiet despair. . . the kind embodied in the expression, "How long, O Lord, how long?"

These "Padre's Hours" were for ranks other than officers, but someone must have listened to the proceedings and made a report. In any event, after the third meeting, I was ordered to come to the office of the Divisional Commander, Major-General Chris Vokes. Shortly after I arrived at Division Headquarters, Padre Roy Durnford of the Seaforths came out of the General's office. He looked very grave indeed, and just nodded his head to me, while making the sign of the cross over me. I never did find out if he was blessing me or giving me the Last Rites. In any case, I prepared for the worst.

Entering the office, I saw that there wasn't a chair set up for me, so I saluted and stood at attention until the General told me to stand at ease. Then it started, "Padre, what the hell is this I hear – that you have been molly-coddling a bunch of malingerers and troublemakers?"

I was totally surprised and totally outraged. The monstrous thought that anyone would dare to question the loyalty of our regiment so infuriated me that I threw caution to the winds and went on the attack. I felt like a bear whose cubs had been attacked. Ordinarily, when I am very angry, I speak in a rather slow and measured way – not this time!

"Sir," I said in a voice that was far too angry and far too loud, "whoever told you that is a damned liar. You know, General Vokes, that the backbone of any regiment are its N.C.O.s. Everything depends on that fact. Most of what I learned in the "Padre's Hour" comes from the sergeants and the bombardiers, and these are no malingerers or troublemakers. In fact, they are the best of the best, but they are getting tired.

"Some of them have children they have never seen who are almost ready to start school. It would be a big improvement, sir, if someone could say to them, 'You'll be home in two years for sure.' These are the N.C.O.s who had kept their men at the guns while the enemy shelled and killed many of them. They no longer have to prove their loyalty – the record takes care of that. But they are tired and fed up, fed up with the cold and the loneliness. They need reassurance that they have not been forgotten."

It seemed that I had been talking a very long time, and I was not particularly happy about the way I conducted the process. The most troubling part of it was that I had no idea what the great man's response would be, but I feared the worst. To my utter surprise, he spoke in a moderate tone, and the anger, so evident in his initial question, was totally absent from his voice.

"Padre, when you are engaging an enemy of your country in war, anything less than total victory in unthinkable. Our division is involved, and will remain involved,

134

until the job is completed. However, you are closer to our men than I am, and they have been here for a long time. I promise you that if the war is not over by the first of November, rotational leave will start immediately. Thank you, Padre, for coming in."

I could hardly believe my ears. It was more than I had dreamed possible. Indeed, I had expected retaliation on a massive scale. I had monopolized the conversation for at least five minutes, and I had used language I had never used before or since to a senior officer. The tone of my voice even frightened me. When it was all over, and I had had time to think, I was reminded of the Duke of Wellington who, when he was discussing his Peninsular Army with a friend, said, "I don't know what effect they have on the enemy, but, by God, they frighten me."

I had listened to this high-pitched voice racing along, barely recognizing it as my own. Then I had received a very fair and reasonable response. After my salute, the General had put out his hand across his desk, we shook hands and I left his office. I found myself trembling like a leaf.

Returning to the regiment, I took a piece of Y.M.C.A. letterhead and wrote a notice to put on the bulletin board:

General Chris Vokes has told me that if the war is not over by November the first of this year, rotational leave to Canada will start as of that date.

Signed – The Padre.

Immediately, the word got around and the place was mobbed. I heard someone say "If Old Electric Whiskers said that, then that's good enough for me." (Old Electric Whiskers was an affectionate nickname, stolen from the

Italian General taken by Wavill's forces, and applied to Vokes because of his moustache.)

In time one of our majors pointed out that I shouldn't have used the C.O.'s notice board without his permission. He said I should have reported to the Colonel and let him write the notice. I replied that this was just part of our "Padre's Hour" procedure. The truth was, having just passed through the valley of the shadow of death, I was in no mood for trifling with any officer, and especially with the one concerned, since he was reputedly the one who had instigated the attempt to have me kicked out of the regiment at the time of the brothel incident. The morale of the regiment rebounded instantly to a new high.

The war dragged on with its chief focus the Western Front. The enemy seemed determined to remain in Italy, and since the alternatives for them were the Western or the Russian fronts, who could blame them? The Fortunate Ridge was fiercely defended by the enemy, and our regiment alone fired sixty-eight thousand shells at enemy positions in one month. As November approached, we were all waiting to see what would come of the promise we had received from the Divisional Commander.

It came in fact a day early. On November 1 we said good-bye to the first member of our regiment to go on leave.

While we were saying good-bye, the enemy fired three shells into our midst, and something very important happened. The gunner going on leave was thrown to the ground by one of his friends who promptly lay on top of him. Others lay on either side of him. It was beautiful. It was the answer of the Third Field Regiment to the integrity of General Chris Vokes; it was an answer to his unswerving trust in our loyalty. We were content.

The General was transferred to command the Fourth Armoured Division on the Western Front. We wished him well, but we regretted losing a commander of honesty and integrity. He could, and did, wipe the floor with subordinates who were slack in their duties. He required, and got, straight answers to his questions. Officers learned that he wanted clear, concise reports, but on the other hand, he was never so insecure that he felt he had to defend his own position. He would change his mind on occasion, as was the case in the matter of the "Padre's Hour" situation. A lesser man might have stood on his dignity. General Vokes, as always, put his command first. I give him full marks for his wisdom, his loyalty to his soldiers and, above all, for his deep compassion. These are the marks of a great leader of men.

24

THE GUNS GO SILENT

Suddenly, in February, we were warned of a move from Italy to the Western Front. Having had all reinforcements cut off, the authorities finally concluded there wasn't any possibility of driving the enemy from their mountain stronghold in Northern Italy.

The first group of gunners sailed from Naples on February 22, 1945. Just before the Third Field left for embarkation at Leghorn for the two-day voyage to Marseilles, we held a regimental memorial service for those who had died serving the Third Field in Sicily and Italy. It was such an impressive service that, years later, it was described in the official history of the Canadian Artillery, *The Gunners of Canada:*

> *With the unit drawn up in hollow square, the service was conducted by the Padre, Honorary Captain Eldon S. Davis, who had crossed the Pocino beaches with the 1st RCHA twenty months before. Lt. Col. Bailey read the Lesson, and after the Padre's address, Regimental Sergeant-Major H.W. Drummond recited the names of the fallen.*

There followed the Last Post, the two minutes of silence, and Reveille. The ceremony concluded with the singing of the National Anthem and the Padre pronouncing the benediction.

To create anonymity on our arrival at Marseilles, all patches and insignia were removed from vehicles and uniforms. But when we entered Orleans, some children standing on a bank as we passed shouted "Vive Canada."

Passing the turnoff to Paris, we proceeded to Belgium and finally on to Holland, arriving just in time to take part in one of the last actions of the war at the Issel River.

Entering the city of Rotterdam, the First Canadian Division was greeted with an incredible outburst of joy which has endeared that great land to Canada for all time.

It had been obvious for days that the war was about to end. One night a game of bridge was in process as the news came over the wireless. Field Marshal Montgomery had just accepted the surrender of all enemy forces on the Western Front.

There was a long pause, and then someone said, "Four spades."

However, the hand was never played. Johnny Westine suddenly got up and danced a little jig and said, "To Hell with the four spades. I got fifty thousand lire for nothing and I didn't even have to die for it." He was referring, of course, to the presale of his job to another gunner in Italy in the event of his death. He fished out a beat-up, old envelope with these words written across it over his signature:

To be opened by the Padre in the event of my death.

POSTSCRIPT

Every soldier's war was peculiarly his own. It was usually made up of a number of events, sometimes with large numbers of people. Sometimes, though, as with a Forward Observation Officer, the war was lonely and solitary, a soldier clinging to his position in a wrecked building or a hole in the ground, while all around the shelling went on hour after endless hour. But, however it happened, it was his war. That is why I have written as I have, telling stories exactly as I saw them, as honestly and frankly as possible.

I have written about making decisions on the spot. Decisions often had to be made quickly and from positions of loneliness, terror or uncertainty. Some decisions were less than the best, and some were as right as could be under the stress of war. Seldom in battle was there an opportunity to ask someone's opinion, and the confidential nature of a padre's position made this nigh impossible. At any rate, I tried to tell it as it was, taking responsibility for every decision I made. Where I have censored my writing, it was to leave out some of the worst parts of a terribly bloody war.

The closer I drew to my regiment and the people around us, the more tolerant I became of their behaviour. When I first came to Italy, I considered her citizens lacking in courage and her soldiers ineffective. Then I met her mountain regiment and knew I was wrong. When I met her resistance fighters I was deeply impressed. I particularly remember a small, dark-haired young woman who seemed to be a leader of her band. She carried eight grenades in her belt. She was not only beautiful but totally dedicated. After she brought vital information to the Canadians, the enemy captured and brutally destroyed her little band. Her casual acceptance of a very violent death made it easy to accept the fact that this beautiful girl was also a totally dedicated soldier. She may well have been the bravest soldier I ever met.

Another feature of the war was that, for many men, time wiped out the worst memories. One man who had served as a Forward Observation Officer, and who had witnessed many of war's horrors, said he could no longer remember or visualize the most bloody of them.

I received three wounds in battle, and all on the same day. Surprised by a sudden shelling, I hastily dug a slit trench, piling the earth on one side of the trench. Then I discovered bedrock ten inches below the surface. There wasn't time to dig another trench, so when the shells came close, I lay down in my shallow refuge and pressed my face against the flat rock, wishing I had been more careful placing the loose earth. The next shell landed five feet from me and just on the outside of the pile of sand. It broke both my eardrums and wounded me twice in the muscles of my back. Had I spread the earth evenly, it would have killed me.

When I reported to the M.O., he said, "Your eardrums

are broken but they don't look too bad. Now, if I send you to hospital you may never get back to the regiment. What would you like me to do?" I answered, "I'd like to stay with the Third Field."

When my ears began to fester, I kept that information to myself. I was totally deaf for about ten days and had to rely on other ears when the shells came in. I was determined to stay with my regiment, even if it meant risking my hearing. Eventually, though, everything cleared up and I was fine.

I spent several years with an ever-changing family of one thousand gunners. And how would I rate these men? Most of them were the very best, and a small few may have been among the worst. I believe our gunners and guns were second to none. That, by the way, was also the view of the enemy. The shelling of the Assoro Ridge, when our gunners laid down a barrage a scant few yards from our infantry, clinging to the perimeter of that lofty town square, enabling assault troops of the Hastings and Prince Edward Regiment to take and hold the town, may have been one of the finest actions of the campaign. When the war was over and won, I remained mighty proud to be a Canadian, and doubly proud to have served with Canadian gunners. Quite simply, I believe they were the best of the best.